Taxcafe.co.uk Tax Guides

How to Avoid Stamp Duty

By Russell Eaton

Important Legal Notices:

TAXCafe™
TAX GUIDE - "How to Avoid Stamp Duty"

Published by:
Taxcafe UK Limited
214 High St
Kirkcaldy, KY1 1JT, UK
Tel: (0044) 01592 560081
Email: team@taxcafe.co.uk

Fourth edition, April 2006

ISBN 1 904608 35 3

Disclaimer

1. This tax guide is sold subject to the condition that neither the publisher nor the author can be held legally responsible for the consequences of any errors or omissions in the book. Please note that this tax guide is intended as general guidance only for individual readers and does NOT constitute legal, accountancy, tax, investment or other professional advice. Taxcafe UK Limited accepts no responsibility or liability for loss which may arise from reliance on information contained in this tax guide.

2. Please note that tax legislation, the law and practices by government and regulatory authorities (e.g. HM Revenue & Customs) are constantly changing. We therefore recommend that for legal, accountancy, tax, investment or other professional advice, you consult a suitably qualified solicitor, accountant, tax specialist, independent financial adviser, or other professional adviser. Please also note that your personal circumstances may vary from the general examples given in this tax guide and your professional adviser will be able to give specific advice based on your personal circumstances.

3. This tax guide covers UK taxation only and any references to 'tax' or 'taxation' in this guide, unless the contrary is expressly stated, refer to UK taxation only. Please note that references to the 'UK' do not include the Channel Islands or the Isle of Man. Foreign tax implications are beyond the scope of this tax guide.

4. Whilst in an effort to be helpful, this guide may refer to general guidance on matters other than UK taxation, Taxcafe UK Limited is not expert in these matters and does not accept any responsibility or liability for loss which may arise from reliance on such information contained in this tax guide.

5. Please note that Taxcafe UK Limited has relied wholly on the expertise of the author in the preparation of the content of this tax guide. The author is not an employee of Taxcafe UK Limited but has been selected by Taxcafe UK Limited using reasonable care and skill to write the content of this tax guide.

Arrangement of Contents

PART ONE covers seven specific strategies for avoiding or reducing stamp duty costs. Each chapter finishes with a section dedicated to selling (rather than buying) property, followed by a short summary.

PART TWO deals with a variety of other stamp duty planning possibilities, including commercial property, and a chapter on the best ways to get on the property ladder.

For Property BUYERS

Several strategies revealed in this book show exactly how to buy residential or non-residential property and reduce the cost of stamp duty. Each easy-to-follow procedure shows how to make savings amounting to thousands of pounds.

But how, you may ask, can you legally avoid paying stamp duty? Just follow the simple step-by-step strategies in this book and you might never have to find money again to pay for stamp duty.

Some of the strategies in this book are widely used by house-building companies. These companies offer incentives such as a lump sum of cash and 'stamp duty paid' deals when you buy a house. This book shows Buyers how to get these same incentives in any house deal!

Little known, but perfectly legal, trade secrets show how you can get big cash incentives and 'stamp duty paid' deals *whoever* you are buying from. The same strategies used by national building companies have been adapted for use by private individuals buying from other private individuals.

A bonus chapter shows the top ten ways to get on the property ladder – this information alone is a 'must read' for anybody contemplating buying property.

So whether you're a professional buy-to-let investor, a developer, or a private individual buying a home, this book is for you. It shows how to buy a property even if you don't have enough money to pay for stamp duty, legal fees, or a mortgage deposit!

*****

Selling Property – Please see next page

For Property SELLERS

Although stamp duty is normally paid by the buyer rather than the seller, some of the strategies in this book can be used by sellers to great effect. For example you can offer certain financial incentives to potential Buyers. Incentives such as 'stamp duty paid' can go a long way to make your property stand out from the crowd.

Better still, when a potential Buyer wishes to negotiate, this book shows how best to get the full asking price, and bag the sale by use of a powerful and unique strategy.

You may well ask *'how can a Seller offer a property free of stamp duty without financial loss?'* The simple step-by-step strategies in this book show exactly how to do this, making it possible to offer a property free of stamp duty whenever you wish.

So whether you're a professional property investor, a developer, or a private individual selling a home, this book is a must. It shows how to offer an irresistible deal to a potential Buyer, and ensure you get a sale at the price you want.

*****

Contents

Contents (cont...)

PART ONE

Stamp Duty Planning Strategies

Introduction to PART ONE

When buying or selling property this book can save you thousands of pounds. When you *buy* a property you could save at least the cost of stamp duty, and when you *sell* you will be able to offer the property free of stamp duty to get a better response (and even a better price). Either way you will win every time.

This book focuses on the buying and selling of property in the UK. PART 1 covers residential property. PART 2 covers other ways of avoiding stamp duty, including land, commercial and non-residential property.

Most of the stamp-duty-planning strategies described in this book cannot be used in property auctions unless you can negotiate direct with the Seller, and have the property withdrawn from auction. Basically, the strategies in this book depend on some kind of direct contact between Buyer and Seller, or their estate agents.

Note that in Scotland, property transactions are often *negotiated* through solicitors. Therefore, if you are buying or selling property in Scotland you are urged to make *direct contact with the Buyer or Seller* as applicable. The fact that conveyancing laws in Scotland are different to the rest of the UK should not affect the principles and strategies covered in this book.

You may be wondering how it is possible to *legally* avoid paying stamp duty on property. Clearly, the tax authorities are not going to be deprived of their tax, and this book does not set out to do this. What we are talking about here is a mix of legal avoidance, paying *less*, and making *savings*. For example, you will see how you can pay nil stamp duty on properties up to £150,000, or how you can legally pay £2,000 in stamp duty instead of, say, £5,000. Or you will learn how you can make savings in property transactions that are equal to or greater than the amount of stamp duty. The net result is that you can usually avoid most or all of the cost of stamp duty.

Using these strategies *Sellers* can also benefit by being able to bridge a price gap. For example, if an offer to buy falls short by £4,000, the Seller can use the strategies in this book to bridge the £4,000 gap without financial loss, and get the full asking price.

2

Several powerful stamp-duty-planning strategies are explained in this book; a kind of à-la-carte menu of tax planning ideas. A brief summary is given at the end of each strategy – but please do not be tempted to just read the summaries as you will miss valuable tips and explanations.

In practice you will be using two or three of these strategies whenever dealing in property, providing substantial savings that are usually worth much more than just the cost of stamp duty. Such strategies are very special and effective, and at least one is likely to work each time you buy or sell a property. If you trade in property professionally such strategies will help to ensure the success of your business.

This book is written as an instruction manual and, as such, it contains step-by-step procedures with easy-to-follow examples. Some points are repeated for added emphasis and to aid comprehension.

To fully appreciate the savings involved let's look at stamp duty costs. The rates of stamp duty are as shown in Fig. 1:

Fig. 1 - Rates of stamp duty

Property Price	Stamp Duty
Not more than £125,000	0%
More than £125,000 but not more than £250,000	1%
More than £250,000 but not more than £500,000	3%
More than £500,000	4%

This means that on a house worth £200,000 you would pay £2,000 in stamp duty. And as soon as you get up to say £300,000, the stamp duty climbs to £9,000! So clearly stamp duty amounts to thousands of pounds, rather than hundreds, and the amounts are of major significance when considering just about any property transaction.

Stamp duty is short for *Stamp Duty Land Tax* and is often abbreviated to SDLT in official documents. In this book we will refer to it simply as 'stamp duty'.

But what exactly is stamp duty? In the context of property or land, stamp duty is nothing more than a property tax. The tax is based on the purchase value of the property.

The tax authorities make no distinction between the property and the fixtures and fittings attached to the property. In other words, fixtures and fittings are also taxable. So if a house is priced at, say, £130,000 and you reckon the fixtures and fittings are worth £5,000, you cannot pay £5,000 separately and change the price to £125,000 to escape stamp duty. This is discussed in more detail in the chapter 'The Threshold Strategy'.

When a Buyer pays stamp duty, the solicitor passes the money onto the tax authorities together with the address of the property. As a property Buyer, you will find that when you get your solicitor's bill, the stamp duty will be listed along with other disbursements such as valuation fees, legal fees, deposits, money transfer costs, and the like. This cannot be avoided but the powerful strategies about to be examined will enable you to recover a large part of these costs in ways unknown to the vast majority of home buyers and sellers.

For simplicity each chapter in PART ONE is written from the point of view of a property **Buyer.** Then at the end of each chapter there is a section titled 'For Property Sellers' which summarizes or adapts the strategy for use by a **Seller.** Please do not be tempted to skip pages or you may miss important information – study each page carefully and it will repay you handsomely.

Clearly, some aspects of the strategies presented here may not apply to each and every property transaction. However, it is certain that some or many aspects of the strategies *will* apply, particularly if you are buying or selling property and are able to deal directly with the Buyer or Seller (or with an estate agent). Therefore, as you read this book you are bound to discover 'golden nuggets' that best apply to your situation, and you will be able to start using them straight away to save a significant amount of money during your property transactions.

In this book the words 'he/his' are used to include 'she/hers'.

Financial Terms Used

Several financial terms referred to in this book come into play when buying or selling property:

1. PRICE.

This is the purchase price agreed with the seller and is the figure entered on all the paperwork (including the Land Registry) as the SELLING PRICE. This is also the figure that will be used by the Lender or Mortgage Company to work out how much money to lend. Note that the PRICE does not include PURCHASE COSTS (see below).

2. PURCHASE COSTS.

- These are the additional costs incurred when buying a property and include legal fees, conveyancing fees, estate agent fees, surveyor costs, valuation costs, council searches, renovation costs, buildings insurance, stamp duty, payments for fixtures, fittings, carpets, furniture and the like.

- Clearly some PURCHASE COSTS may not apply to a particular purchase but others will always apply, the point being: PURCHASE COSTS cannot normally be included in the loan or mortgage. You have to find the money for PURCHASE COSTS from personal savings or other sources.

3. LOAN.

This is the amount of money borrowed to buy a property (referred to as the mortgage or loan). The amount of the LOAN is based on the PRICE. For example, a 95% LTV (Loan To Value) means that you get a loan that is equivalent to 95% of the PRICE. The expression *Loan To Value* is used (rather than Loan To Price) because Lenders base the amount of the loan on the <u>valuation</u> that they carry out before giving you the money. Provided that the valuation is not *lower* than the PRICE, you will get a loan based on the PRICE. In the United Kingdom you can typically get LOANS that vary between 70% and 100% of the PRICE. If the LOAN is 100% you will borrow an amount of money equal to the PRICE, and hence not have to pay a deposit.

4. DEPOSIT.

This is the amount paid towards the PRICE. For example, if you get a 95% LOAN, the deposit is the balance of 5%. Where funds are scarce a person will naturally opt for as big a LOAN as possible, thus minimizing the DEPOSIT.

5. CONVEYANCING COSTS.

These relate to the legal fees, valuation fees, council searches, stamp duty, and other costs applied by your solicitor or conveyancer.

Normally, the amount of the LOAN does not take into account any CONVEYANCING COSTS; in other words, you cannot ask the Lender to give you extra money for CONVEYANCING COSTS. The terms LEGAL COSTS and CONVEYANCING COSTS are interchangeable in this book.

Clearly there is an overlap between the PURCHASE COSTS and the CONVEYANCING COSTS in the sense that many of the same costs come under both headings. The point to keep in mind is that some PURCHASE COSTS are not channelled through the solicitor, e.g. you may agree to buy some furniture from the Seller by paying for it directly without involving the solicitor. The stamp duty is shown under two headings: PURCHASE COSTS *and* CONVEYANCING COSTS. Typically, the Buyer will pay the stamp duty to the solicitor (this is not normally included in the LOAN), and the solicitor will pay it on to HM Revenue & Customs with details of the address. There is no legal way to avoid the payment of stamp duty when a property transaction requires that stamp duty be applied. However, this book shows how this cost can be recovered (or reduced), so that in effect you end up not incurring the cost of stamp duty.

The seven stamp-duty-planning strategies that follow are shown in Fig.2 (on the next page).

Fig. 2 - The Seven Stamp Duty Planning Strategies

1	The Tax Exemption Strategy
2	The Threshold Strategy
3	The Link Strategy
4	The Mortgage Cashback Strategy
5	The Price Strategy
6	The Valuation Strategy
7	The Combination Strategy

The Tax Exemption Strategy

In the UK there are about two thousand 'Designated Disadvantaged Areas' (DDAs) spread all over the country, although there are not many in the more affluent shires of south-east England. Glasgow, for example, has many DDAs. The point is this: if a residential property is purchased in a DDA, no stamp duty applies if the value is not over £150,000. If the value is over £150,000 the normal rules apply.

Note: Stamp duty rules for commercial property (i.e. non-residential property) are the same, whether located in a DDA or not. In other words, there is no stamp duty relief for commercial property by virtue of being located in a DDA.

It is not, of course, being suggested that you buy a residential property in a DDA in order to escape stamp duty! But it is worth checking whether the property you want to buy is in a DDA. If it is not, this particular strategy cannot be applied. If the property *is* in a DDA, it means that you can buy the property completely free of stamp duty if the value is not over £150,000.

DDAs are also referred to as *Enterprise Areas* because the government wants to encourage economic growth in such areas (hence the stamp duty concession).

To see a list of DDAs (too many to list here) go to:
http://www.hmrc.gov.uk/so/disadvantaged.htm

Alternatively, go to:
http://www.hmrc.gov.uk/so/pcode_search.htm

which allows postcodes to be entered to check if within a DDA.

You can also enquire about DDAs or *Enterprise Areas* by phoning the Stamp Taxes Helpline on 0845 603 0135. Poor or neglected areas are clearly more likely to be in a DDA than millionaires' row.

TIP

Solicitors usually add about £50-£70 to their conveyancing fees charged to the Buyer for arranging payment of stamp duty. The Buyer can save this money by arranging this payment himself. Simply go to http://www.hmrc.gov.uk/so/sdlt_website.htm and follow the on-screen instructions. Note that you can complete and submit the stamp duty payment form online. Alternatively, telephone the Inland Revenue, 0845 302 1472, and obtain the forms for paying stamp duty by post. Remember to tell your solicitor that you will be filling in and making the SDLT payment direct to Inland Revenue and you therefore do not want to be charged for this service. The form is simple to fill in, and easy-to-follow guidance notes are given with the form. If you get stuck, you can telephone Inland Revenue for guidance (0845 603 0135). The form should be filled in and submitted <u>after completion</u> of purchase because the date of completion must be entered on the form. Therefore, you will need to receive a completion statement from your solicitor before completing the form. Before deciding whether to do it yourself, have a look at a blank form and the guidance notes that come with it.

You probably won't get the stamp duty exemption unless you ask for it, and more often than not home buyers do not ask. There have been many cases of people paying stamp duty unnecessarily in DDAs and never getting refunds. This happens because some solicitors may not be aware of the tax exemption and because the tax authorities do not automatically check stamp duty payments against DDA records to give refunds.

Apart from DDAs (and for the sake of completeness) it should be mentioned that *registered charities* are exempt from stamp duty. The law on this goes back to the *Parsonage Act of 1938* but is now enshrined in current stamp duty legislation.

Note that if a registered charity sells a property, the buyer is not exempt from stamp duty by virtue of the *Seller* being a registered charity. In other words, the exemption only applies to a Buyer who is a registered charity. So, for example, if a private person buys a church from a registered charity there is no stamp duty exemption. But if a registered charity buys a house from a private individual the stamp duty exemption applies.

It is not being suggested that you become a registered charity for the purpose of avoiding stamp duty. However, if you are in any event planning to become a registered charity, it makes sense to buy any property after receiving your charity registration number.

If claiming stamp duty relief *after* you or your solicitor has paid it, there is a two-year cut off date for reimbursements. This means you must claim a refund from Inland Revenue within two years of purchase.

Using *The Tax Exemption Strategy*

This strategy can be adapted for a Seller. That is, a property can be offered for sale 'free of stamp duty' if it qualifies for stamp duty exemption by being in a DDA. This can be important in the initial stages of attracting Buyer attention.

A registered charity cannot offer a property 'free of stamp duty' by virtue of the Seller's charity status. However, there is nothing to stop a registered charity offering a property free of stamp duty by using some of the strategies in this book. And of course, if a property is being sold to a registered charity, it can be offered 'free of stamp duty' since the Buyer would be exempt.

When selling a property exempt from stamp duty it is important for both the Buyer and Seller to tell their respective solicitors that a stamp duty exemption applies as this is not automatically checked by solicitors or the tax authorities.

For a complete list of stamp duty tax exemptions (referred to by Inland Revenue as 'Stamp Duty Land tax reliefs') go to the government website at:

www.hmrc.gov.uk/manuals/sdltmanual/SDLTM20010.htm

This provides a list of the various tax concessions available in regard to stamp duty. For example, item SDLTM29000 tell you that where a purchase is made by a crofting community, stamp duty savings may be available on that purchase. You can then follow the prompts to get full details for that item.

Summary of *The Tax Exemption Strategy*

1. In the UK there are many DDAs (Designated Disadvantaged Areas). Any property bought in a DDA is exempt from stamp duty if the value is not over £150,000.

2. DDAs tend to be more common in poor or neglected areas, in both rural and urban communities. To check if a property might be located in a DDA telephone 0845 603 0135, or go to *http://www.hmrc.gov.uk/so/disadvantaged.htm*

3. If taking advantage of a property located in a DDA be sure to tell your solicitor in case you are entitled to avoid stamp duty.

4. Whenever selling a property that qualifies for tax exemption always consider offering the property 'free of stamp duty'.

The Threshold Strategy

This strategy is about not paying a higher rate of stamp duty unless you legally have to. For properties priced close to the first threshold of £125,000 it may be possible to pay no stamp duty at all.

As mentioned, the rates of stamp duty are as follows:

Property Price	Stamp Duty
Not more than £125,000	0%
More than £125,000 but not more than £250,000	1%
More than £250,000 but not more than £500,000	3%
More than £500,000	4%

In this strategy we will be concerned with three tax thresholds:

- Paying nil duty instead of 1% duty.

- Paying 1% duty instead of 3% duty.

- Paying 3% duty instead of 4% duty.

For instance, a property priced at £250,000 incurs stamp duty at 1% (£2,500). But a property priced at £250,001 incurs stamp duty at 3% (£7,500.03 which is always rounded up to the nearest £5, ie £7,505). So just by moving down to a lower threshold by making a small change in the price, the potential savings can amount to thousands of pounds.

It therefore does not make sense to buy a property priced just over the threshold of £250,000. In fact you will rarely find properties priced in the £251,000-£260,000 bracket precisely for this reason. A similar analogy applies to the £500,000 threshold.

In practice, Estate Agents and Sellers tend to avoid offering prices in the £250-£260,000 bracket, but you sometimes see prices at £259,000 or £260,000. The first £15,000 after the threshold tends to be 'forbidden territory'. In other words there are few properties priced between £250,000 and £265,000. This can be verified by looking in any property newspaper and in estate agents' windows.

We can take advantage of this. Fig.3 shows how.

Fig. 3 - The Thresholds

OMV = Open Market Value
THRESHOLDS = £125,000 or £250,000 or £500,000, whichever applies most to your property deal.

Item	Seller's Perceived OMV (£)	Seller's asking price (£)	Potential price reduction (£)
1	Under the threshold	Under the threshold	May or may not be negotiable
2	Less than 2% over the threshold	The threshold price	Not very negotiable
3	Between 2% and 4% over the threshold	Between 2% and 4% over the threshold	Very negotiable
4	Between 4% and 10% over the threshold	Between 4% and 10% over the threshold	Not very negotiable
5	More than 10% over the threshold	More than 10% over the threshold	The threshold strategy becomes irrelevant

Item 1 in Fig. 3 shows that if the Seller/agent thinks the OMV (Open Market Value) is, for example, under £250,000, the stamp duty threshold of £250,000 is irrelevant and the price may or may not be negotiable.

Item 2 in Fig. 3 shows that if the Seller/agent thinks the OMV is, for example, £253,000 a price reduction is unlikely to be granted as the price has already been reduced to £250,000 to bring it below the stamp duty threshold.

Items 3 in Fig 3 show that if the Seller/agent thinks the OMV is, for example, £257,000, and the asking price is £257,000, there is a good chance of negotiating the price down to £250,000 because the Seller/agent knows this will save the Buyer significant stamp duty. In another example, if the Seller/agent thinks the OMV is, £130,000 and the asking price is £130,000, there is a good chance of negotiating the price down to £125,000 and avoiding stamp duty altogether.

Item 4 in Fig. 3 shows that if the Seller/agent thinks the OMV is, for example, £267,500 a price reduction to £250,000 is unlikely to be granted because it would be too big a reduction. The Seller/agent has decided to not take the stamp duty threshold into account in setting a selling price as it would be too much of a 'sacrifice'. However, there is still the possibility of negotiating a discount, but not enough to reach the lower threshold.

Item 5 in Fig 3 shows that if the Seller/agent thinks the OMV is, for example, £280,000, a price reduction to £250,000 is likely to be out of the question, and therefore the threshold strategy cannot be used.

The strategy then is to shortlist properties priced *over the threshold* but within about 4% of the threshold price. For example, any properties between £129,000 and £135,000 offer good chances of negotiating a price reduction down to £125,000. Similarly, for properties between £251,000 and £260,000. Or between £500,000 and £520,000.

Also remember that properties offered at just below the tax threshold, e.g. £249,500, may well have been reduced from a higher price in order to get a sale *without stamp duty being an objection*. Therefore, properties priced in this way may offer good value for money.

14

Here is an example of how the negotiation might go:

Example

Buyer: *'You are selling the house for £259,000 is that correct?'*

Seller: *'Yes, the price is £259,000 and includes all the fixtures and fittings already discussed.'*

Buyer: *'Well, as you may know I would have to pay £7,770 in stamp duty on a price of £259,000 so I have a proposition. May I explain my proposed offer?'*

Seller: *'Please go ahead, I'm always open to offers.'*

Buyer: *'If I buy your house for £259,000 I will have to pay £7,770 stamp duty (and that's without taking into account solicitor fees, valuation fees, and the like). I therefore want to ask if you can accept £250,000?* [Explain the stamp duty implications]. *If you can agree to this, I will buy a list of chattels from your house for £5,000. This means you will get a total sum of £255,000 for your house.'*

Seller: *'Assuming we can agree a list of contents, how would you pay me the £5,000?'*

Buyer: *'My solicitor will confirm to your solicitor that I have agreed to buy a list of chattels from you, and the additional £5,000 would be paid upon completion. So you will get the £5,000 on the same day that the completion of sale goes through.'*

Seller: *'That sounds good. We may have a deal. Let's talk about the list of chattels.'*

Here are some tips for preparing the list of chattels:

- Take care that any amounts allocated to 'Chattels', such as carpets and curtains, are properly supportable. So in this example, the items listed need to reflect a realistic value of £5,000 in the eyes of the tax authorities. Of course, the Seller may only give the items a value of £500. The lower the perceived value for the Seller the better, as the £5,000 will then be more highly appreciated.

- Fixtures and fittings are not allowed as they are taxable. Therefore, only chattels (things that can be moved) are allowable.

- The list must be genuine, and the goods on the list must exist, even though the transaction might be viewed as a vehicle for paying money to the Seller (in this example, £5,000). The Buyer should not try to 'get his money's worth'. Rather, he should try to help the Seller find the right balance between a worthless list and a supportable list.

- As many items as possible should be included on the list, however inconsequential and small the value. For example, include, if possible, all kitchen appliances and equipment. The longer the list the better.

- Do not enter money values for each item. Only enter the total value (e.g. £5,000).

- Do not enter terms such as 'fixtures and fittings' or 'floor coverings' or 'kitchen appliances' or 'Chattels'. Avoid generic names. Enter an individual name/description for each item.

WARNING

The UK tax authorities do not like property transactions that include a large payment for 'chattels' (also known as 'movables') as a way of avoiding stamp duty. In particular they are likely to challenge and investigate a payment for chattels if the amount exceeds 10% of the price of the property. To play safe, any payment for chattels should not exceed 5% of the price of the property. Furthermore, the items sold as chattels must be worth the amount paid. Therefore, the more substantive the list of items the better.

In the above example the buyer would pay £257,500 for the house (£250,000 plus 1% stamp duty, plus £5,000). This compares against £266,770 without a reduction (£259,000 plus 3% stamp duty). So, as a result of negotiating a lower price, a saving of £9,270 has been made!

Note that the Seller ended up getting £255,000 instead of £259,000, a mere difference of £4,000 compared with the buyer's savings of £9,270.

Is it legal to offer to buy chattels in this way? Yes it is, provided the chattels are genuine. This is what the tax authorities have to say on the matter (the following is a summarized extract from Revenue and Customs):

"For an item to be regarded as a fixture as opposed to a chattel (called 'movable' in Scotland), the item must be fixed to the property. Where a purchaser agrees to buy a property for a price that includes an amount properly attributed to chattels, that amount will not be charged to Stamp Duty.

In recent times an increasing number of cases have arisen in which the amount of money attributed to chattels is more than a small percentage of the total amount. This has been particularly noticeable where the chargeable amount is brought just below the £250,000 or £500,000 stamp duty thresholds.

Under the Stamp Duty regime a "just and reasonable apportionment" is required where a price is paid partly for a property and partly for chattels. It does not matter that the parties to a transaction may agree a particular apportionment, which is then documented in the contract. The apportionment will not be correct unless it was arrived at on a "just and reasonable" basis.

The Inland Revenue has the right to make enquiries into the property transaction and into cases where a deduction has been made for chattels, to confirm that those items properly fall within the definition of chattels. The Inland Revenue is unable to provide a comprehensive list of items that it accepts as chattels because each case must be considered on its own merits and because this is an area of the law that continues to evolve.

The following are, however, confirmed as being items that will normally be regarded as chattels:

- *Carpets (fitted or otherwise).*
- *Curtains and Blinds.*
- *Free-standing furniture.*

- *Kitchen white goods.*

- *Electric and Gas fires (provided that they can be removed by disconnection from the power supply without causing damage to the property).*

- *Light shades and fittings (unless recessed).*

- *Plants and shrubs growing in pots or containers (internally or externally).*

The following will not normally be regarded as chattels:

- *Fitted kitchen units and cupboards (whether or not they are standing loose, unless they were designed to stand loose).*

- *Gas ovens and wall-mounted ovens.*

- *Fitted kitchen sinks bathroom sanitary ware, even if standing loose.*

- *Central heating systems.*

- *Intruder alarm systems.*

- *Plants, shrubs or trees growing in the soil."*

It is clear, then, that the tax authorities will allow a separate payment from Buyer to Seller for chattels provided that any stamp duty avoidance is incidental to the transaction rather than the sole purpose. It is also clear that such chattels may include fitted carpets, white kitchen goods, fitted curtains, removable gas and electric fires, and many items which traditionally have been thought of as 'fixtures and fittings'.

In fact the term 'fixtures and fittings' should never come into the transaction at any point, as matters can get confused. It is best to only think in terms of chattels (or 'movables' in Scotland).

There is a misconception that the value of fixtures and fittings must be accounted for and added to the price of the property for stamp duty purposes. This is not so. The tax authorities regard fixtures and fittings as a taxable part of the property. If fixtures and fittings are charged for separately this cost must be added to the selling price, and stamp duty will be payable on the grand total. Therefore, the tax authorities do not care whether fixtures and fittings are included in the price or charged for separately since it makes no difference to the amount of tax paid.

In practice, fixtures and fittings will normally be included in the selling price and therefore do not need to be 'evaluated'. However, the fixtures and fittings do need to be listed and agreed so that there can be no misunderstanding over what the Seller is or is not leaving behind. This is standard practice, and solicitors use a ready-made check list when agreeing fixtures and fittings.

The point about *The Threshold Strategy* is that fixtures and fittings cannot be used as a means of paying money to the Seller, *but chattels can.* This is what it boils down to:

- A Buyer gets taxed on non-chattels (i.e. fixtures) and they cannot be used to negotiate a below-threshold price.

- A Buyer does not get taxed on chattels and they can be used to negotiate a below-threshold price (but to be safe don't pay more than 5% of the selling price for chattels).

- Make sure that as many items as possible are listed as chattels rather than as fixtures and fittings. That way the chattels list will be more substantial and acceptable to the tax authorities.

A final point to remember is this: *Generally, be inclined to ask for a price reduction on any property priced over the threshold, but within about 4% of the threshold. They provide opportunities for good price reductions. Knowing this valuable tip can save you thousands of pounds.*

Using *The Threshold Strategy* for Selling Property

This strategy can be used to effect by a Seller as a means of securing a sale or a higher price. The Seller does this by helping the Buyer pay less stamp duty on the property you are selling, to your mutual benefit. More specifically, this strategy helps the Buyer legally avoid paying a higher rate of stamp duty than necessary.

As mentioned at the beginning of this chapter, it does not make sense to sell a property priced just over the threshold of £250,000 as this is likely to create Buyer resistance. In fact you will rarely find properties priced in the £251,000-£260,000 bracket precisely for this reason.

The strategy for the Seller is to avoid offering a property for sale that is priced close to but over the threshold, *unless you are willing to come down in price.*

For example, don't offer a property for sale at £130,000 unless you offer it subject to negotiation and 'free of stamp duty'. You can then reduce the price to £125,000 to enable the buyer to avoid stamp duty. If you offer the property for sale at a fixed price of £129,000 or £130,000 you will create strong Buyer resistance as Buyers will want to bring the price down to £125,000 in order to avoid paying 1% stamp duty. It is better to sell at £125,000, or if you think it is worth more, then £140,000.

Here is an example of how the negotiation might go. Let's assume you think your house is worth at least £260,000, but you are keen to sell. You therefore offer the house at £259,000. As this is £9,000 above the tax threshold, you know you are bound to be asked to reduce the price to £250,000, but for you this is too little. In the example that follows we will assume you are willing to accept £255,000 as your rock-bottom price.

Example

Buyer: *You are selling the house for £259,000 is that correct?*

Seller: *Yes, the price is £259,000 and includes all the fixtures and fittings already discussed.*

Buyer: *Would you be willing to reduce the price to £250,000 as this would save me a lot of money in stamp duty.*

Seller: *Yes, I understand that you would save stamp duty by only paying 1% instead of 3%, so I have a special proposition. May I explain it to you?*

Buyer: *Okay, what do you have in mind?*

Seller: *Well, if you were to buy the house for £259,000 you would have to pay £7,770 in stamp duty. If your buy the house at £250,000 the stamp duty is only £2,500, so I want to suggest a compromise. I am willing to sell the house at £250,000 so that you can save stamp duty costs. But additionally, I want you to agree to buy a list of chattels from me amounting to £5,000.*

Buyer: *This sounds interesting. So what is the total amount I would pay? Would it be £250,000 plus £2,500 stamp duty, plus £5,000 for chattels?*

Seller: *Yes, the total would be £257,500. Let me go through the list of chattels with you so that you can decide what to do.*

(Later)

Buyer: *If I agree to this, how would the money for the chattels be handed over?*

Seller: *My solicitor will confirm to your solicitor that I have agreed to sell a list of chattels, and the additional £5,000 would be paid by your solicitor upon completion. Do we have a deal? If so, I will confirm in writing the list of chattels so that we all know what is being left behind at the property.*

Buyer: *That sounds good. We may have a deal. Let's finalize the list of chattels.*

In the above example the buyer would pay £257,500 for the house (£250,000 plus 1% stamp duty, plus £5,000). This compares against £266,770 without a reduction (£259,000 plus 3% stamp duty). So, as a result of using this strategy, the Seller has made a sale and saved the Buyer £9,270!

Of course, you ended up getting £255,000 instead of the £259,000 asking price, but that's better than £250,000, and you can move on with your life.

Is it legal to offer to sell chattels in this way? Yes, as mentioned, it is perfectly legal provided the chattels are genuine. The point here is that fixtures and fittings cannot be used as a means of receiving money from the Buyer, *but chattels can.*

Summary of *The Threshold Strategy*:

1. Use The Threshold Strategy to negotiate significant price reductions. .

2. Shortlist several properties that meet your criteria and fall within the chosen price threshold. Prepare the figures to be negotiated, and negotiate direct with the Seller. If an estate

agent is involved, ask the agent to let you negotiate direct with the Seller (assure the agent that he will not be bypassed in any way and that his agency commission will not be affected). If this is not possible, try to do it through a telephone conference with all three parties on the line. As a last resort negotiate with the Seller through the estate agent.

3. Prepare a CHATTELS LIST by walking around the property and making notes – this is a list of things that you can pay for separately (see above chapter). The longer the list the better. Make sure that no possible chattels get included on the 'fixtures and fittings' list prepared by the solicitor. Use the chattels list in your negotiations. Think of the chattels list as a vehicle for paying money to the Seller.

4. Consider your property budget (the price range you can pay) and establish which stamp duty threshold is most applicable. Then keep an eye on the property market for properties priced just over the threshold. Do this to seek out opportunities to negotiate good price reductions.

5. If selling property, use the strategy to secure a better price: offer the property at a price that is **higher** than the stamp duty threshold, but free of stamp duty. And then be willing to negotiate a lower price, which may or may not include selling chattels. You would offer to reduce the price as a negotiating stance and to help the Buyer avoid or reduce the amount of stamp duty.

6. A Seller should always consider the possibility of selling chattels by preparing a chattels list in advance. This is a list of movable things that can be offered to a Buyer in return for a sum of money. The longer the list the better. Make sure that no possible chattels get included on the 'fixtures and fittings' list prepared by the solicitor. Use the chattels list in your negotiations. Think of the chattels list as a vehicle for receiving money from the Buyer.

The Link Strategy

This strategy could reduce the amount of stamp duty from 4% to 3%, from 3% to 1% (or even from 4% to 1%), giving a huge potential saving. It will only suit a property Buyer who may want to buy more than one property from the same Seller, either as a lot, or as a series of transactions over time. It will also suit anybody buying at auction.

The Link Strategy helps you avoid falling into a *stamp duty tax trap*, a trap that most people have never heard of. Just about every week of the year people fall into this tax trap and end up paying much more stamp duty than they need to.

The Tax Trap

If buying two or more properties from the same person or company there is a likelihood that the transaction will be regarded as 'linked' for stamp duty tax purposes. This is so even if there is a time gap between each property transaction. For example, if buying two properties each priced at £150,000, the stamp duty rate would be 3% for each property rather than 1% (because, in this example, the total of £300,000 is above the stamp duty threshold of £250,000). In this example, the *extra* stamp duty you pay is £6,000. By using *The Link Strategy*, you can potentially make savings of tens of thousands of pounds, depending on the prices of the properties.

As you can see, when the linked rule comes into play the extra stamp duty paid can be very substantial. If there is any possibility that you will be buying further properties from the same source (at any future date) or more than one property from the same person, it is important to be aware of *linked transactions* (the tax trap).

Section 108 of *The Finance Act 2003* has a section titled 'Linked Transactions' which reads as follows:

108 Linked transactions

(1) Transactions are "linked" for the purposes of this Part if they form part of a single scheme, arrangement or series of transactions between the same vendor and purchaser or, in either case, persons connected with them.

Section 839 of the Taxes Act 1988 (connected persons) has effect for the purposes of this subsection

(2) Where there are two or more linked transactions with the same effective date, the purchaser, or all of the purchasers if there is more than one, may make a single land transaction return as if all of those transactions that are notifiable were a single notifiable transaction.

(3) Where two or more purchasers make a single return in respect of linked transactions, section 103 (joint purchasers) applies as if-
(a) the transactions in question were a single transaction, and
(b) those purchasers were purchasers acting jointly.

What this means is that if you are buying more than one property from the same Seller, then according to *The Finance Act 2003*, the transactions could be linked and you will have to pay stamp duty *at a rate* based on the *total value* of all the properties being purchased.

However, there are circumstances when there may be no linkage even though you may be buying more than one property from the same person or company. And when there is no linkage you do not get clobbered with extra stamp duty! What are these circumstances? Here are some examples:

Example 1.

A house builder is selling flats. He makes a special offer: *'Buy two flats and you get a discount of 15% on the second flat'*. Peter buys the two flats and *benefits* from the discount. This kind of transaction is linked because they are both part of the same business deal. The stamp duty rate is therefore based on the total value of both flats (resulting in a big jump in stamp duty!).

Alternative scenario.

A house builder is selling flats. He makes a special offer: 5% discount plus stamp duty paid. Peter buys one flat on these terms. Then a week later (or a month later, or a year later) Peter sees an advertisement from the builder offering further flats for sale, based on the same terms: 5% discount plus stamp duty paid. Peter responds to the advertisement in writing, making reference to the advertisement, and making no reference to any other property deals. In this alternative scenario there is no link because there was *no awareness* of further flats being available until Peter saw the advertisement. When it came to buying the second property, the Buyer *did not benefit* from his association with the first property deal or with the Seller because he got no special terms based on a second purchase. In this alternative scenario the two key phrases are *no awareness* and *no benefit*. When there is *no awareness* and *no benefit*, there is no link.

Example 2.

A house builder is selling flats. He sells a flat to Peter for £150,000. Peter is so pleased with the deal that he goes back to the builder a month later and buys a second flat. This kind of transaction is linked because they are both part of the same business deal, or series of business deals. Peter's decision to buy a second flat is *linked* to his awareness of the first flat. The time gap of a month is immaterial – what counts here is the fact that the Buyer had knowledge that linked both transactions. When Peter bought the second flat he *benefited* from his knowledge of the first flat and from his association with the Seller. The stamp duty rate is therefore based on the total value of both flats. This means a portion of the stamp duty payable is 'backdated' to the first property.

Alternative scenario.

Let's suppose that the house builder sells a flat to Peter at £150,000. Peter is so pleased with the flat that he asks a friend to act as a scout and find him another flat in a similar price range. Peter has complete confidence in his friend and gives him full discretion to put down a reservation fee if he finds the right property. His friend does indeed find a great property and pays the reservation fee of £500. Peter is happy with this second deal but discovers a week later that the Seller is, by coincidence, the same person that sold him the first flat. In this alternative scenario there is no link because there was *no awareness* of the common ownership. Furthermore, Peter can provide documentary evidence showing that he instructed his friend to act for him. When it came to buying the second property, the Buyer *did not benefit* from his acquaintance with the owner of the first property. Once again, if there is *no awareness* and *no benefit*, there is no link.

Example 3.

John is a developer and he sells a house to Peter. About a year later, John contacts Peter and tells him he has another good property to offer him; this time it's a flat. Peter buys the flat and rents it out. This kind of transaction is linked because they are both part of a series of business deals. The one-year time gap is immaterial. The stamp duty rate is therefore based on the total value of the house and the flat. This means a higher rate of stamp duty, and a portion of the stamp duty payable is 'backdated' to the first property.

Alternative scenario.

John is a developer and he sells a house to Peter. About a year later Peter decides he would like to buy a flat to rent out. He places an advertisement in the *property wanted* section of a suitable newspaper. John happens to see the advertisement and replies to it in writing, making reference to the advertisement. A deal is negotiated and Peter buys the flat without any reference to the house that he also purchased from John a year ago. In this alternative scenario there is no link because there was *no awareness* of the common ownership until John replied to the advertisement.

Furthermore, Peter can provide documentary evidence showing that he advertised for a property and that John responded *in writing* to the advertisement. When it came to buying the second property, the Buyer *did not benefit* from his acquaintance with the owner of the first property. Yet again, when there is *no awareness* and *no benefit*, there is no link.

Example 4.

Peter buys a bungalow from John's building firm. A year later Peter sees an advertisement from John's firm offering a flat for sale. Peter responds to the advertisement without remembering that a year earlier he had dealt with the same firm for the purchase of his bungalow. Peter has not benefited from any discounts or special offers even though he is buying from John for the second time. In fact, Peter got exactly the same terms as if he were buying from John for the first time (absolutely no special terms whatsoever).

This kind of transaction is linked because they are both part of a series of business deals. The one-year time gap is immaterial. The stamp duty rate is therefore based on the total value of the bungalow and the flat. This means a portion of the stamp duty payable is 'backdated' to the first bungalow. Peter cannot argue that he did not benefit from, and was not aware of, the common ownership. The fact is that the two deals are linked by virtue of having the same Seller, and Peter cannot prove otherwise. Without documentary proof you have no case because a 'linked transaction' is assumed unless you can prove otherwise.

Alternative scenario.

Peter buys a bungalow from John's building firm. A year later Peter goes to a property auction and buys a flat from John. Later Peter discovers that the flat bought at auction was owned by the same John that sold him a bungalow a year ago. Clearly, Peter was not aware that John was the owner at the time of bidding for the property, and clearly Peter never suggested to John that he should sell the flat at auction. In this alternative scenario there is no link because there was *no awareness* of the common ownership. When it came to buying the second property at auction, the Buyer *did not benefit* from his association with the first property or with the

Seller. In this alternative scenario the two key phrases are *no awareness* and *no benefit*. When there is *no awareness* and *no benefit*, there is no link.

Example 5.

Peter is interested in buying two run-down flats in a city centre building. He checks them out through the estate agent and is informed *in writing* that they are both owned by *City Banking Corporation*, as a result of a repossession. Peter goes to the property auction and successfully bids for the first flat. He decides he will try his luck and go for the second flat, and again he wins the bid. This kind of transaction is linked because they are both part of a succession of business deals. In any investigation by the tax authorities they will quickly discover that the estate agent informed Peter about the common ownership of the two flats. The stamp duty rate is therefore based on the total value of both flats (resulting in a big jump in stamp duty!).

Alternative scenario.

Peter is interested in buying two run-down flats in a city centre building. He checks them out through the estate agent but is not told who the owner is or that they both belong to the same owner. There is nothing in the paperwork or the auction house brochure to indicate that both flats have a common owner. Peter buys both properties at auction.

Later he discovers that both properties were owned by the *City Banking Corporation*. In this alternative scenario there is no link because there was *no awareness* of the common ownership. When it came to buying the second property at auction, the Buyer *did not benefit* from knowing he had just bought the first flat. In this alternative scenario the two key phrases are *no awareness* and *no benefit*. When there is *no awareness* and *no benefit*, there is no link.

Example 6.

Peter wants to buy two flats from John. For buying two flats Peter gets a special 5% discount on each flat. This is a linked transaction so stamp duty is paid at 3% instead of 1%. However, by getting 5% discount Peter is better off even though he has to pay the additional stamp duty. Peter therefore goes ahead with the deal on the basis of it being a linked transaction.

Alternative scenario.

Peter wants to buy two flats from John. However, he decides that he will buy just one flat and he negotiates a 10% discount. A week later Peter sees an advertisement from a person called John and as a result of *seeing the advertisement* Peter decides to buy another flat. He tells his solicitor in writing that as a result of seeing the advertisement he wants to buy a property from a person called John (throughout the proceedings Peter and John make no reference to any other property deals). So Peter goes ahead and buys the second flat *without any discount*. Each transaction has been 'negotiated' separately with nothing to link them. Peter did *not use his awareness* of the first transaction to derive a benefit from the second transaction: as no discount was given *no benefit* was obtained. Furthermore, at the time of buying the first property, Peter *did not contemplate* buying a second property. As this is not a linked transaction, stamp duty is only paid at the rate of 1% (rather than 3%) for each property. The net result is that Peter bought two properties, paid stamp duty at 1%, and obtained a 10% discount on one of them.

Example 7.

This example shows how a Buyer can use *The Link Strategy* to buy two or more properties from the same Seller, without falling into the *linked transaction* trap (and with financial gain for both parties).

Scenario A (not using the strategy):

Peter has been watching a property development and wants to invest in a new-build block. The price of each flat is £160,000. Peter negotiates with the Seller and agrees to buy two flats at £150,000 each. As this is a linked transaction the Buyer pays

£300,000, plus stamp duty at 3% = £9,000. The Seller receives £300,000.

The total costs for Buyer and Seller are as follows:

Table A

Total costs incurred by Buyer	Total money received by Seller
Two flats at £150,000 each = £300,000	Two flats at £150,000 each = £300,000
Plus stamp duty @ 3% = £9,000	(Stamp duty of £9,000 paid by Buyer)
TOTAL: £309,000	TOTAL: £300,000

Alternative Scenario B:

Peter has been watching a property development and wants to invest in a new-build block. The asking price of each flat is £160,000. Peter negotiates with the Seller and this is what happens:

- Peter buys one flat only at the full asking price of £160,000.

- The Seller agrees to pay the cost of stamp duty amounting to £1,600.

- The Seller also agrees to give the Buyer a cash incentive amounting to £7,000 (this is less than 5% of the price).

- The deal goes through as a single unconditional transaction (it is not part of any kind of multiple deal and no reference is made to the possibility that further business will transpire).

- Later (say two weeks later), Peter is surprised to see an advertisement stating that another flat has become available from the Seller. Alternatively, the Buyer is surprised to receive a letter from a friend telling him about an opportunity to buy a flat. As a result of this (documented) turn of events, Peter goes ahead and buys a second property on the same terms as before. This means two separate transactions have taken place with no linkage in terms of benefits and awareness between the two transactions.

- The total cost for Buyer and Seller would therefore be as shown in Table B:

Table B

Total costs incurred by Buyer	Total money received by Seller
Two flats at £160,000 each = £320,000	Two flats at £160,000 each = £320,000
(Stamp duty of £3,200 is paid by Seller)	Less stamp duty @ 1% = £3,200
Less £14,000 cash incentives = £14,000	Less £14,000 cash incentive = £14,000
TOTAL: £306,000	TOTAL: £302,800

- This means the Seller would get £2,800 more than otherwise, plus he would be able to offer a similar package to other customers if he wished to, as a way of generating more business.

- The buyer would benefit by paying a total of £306,000 instead of £309,000, plus having the flexibility to give the Seller repeat business without getting clobbered with excessive stamp duty.

Note: The cash incentive would be paid by the Seller to the Buyer from the proceeds of sale. This would be done on completion of sale by the Seller's solicitor. If buying with a mortgage, the Buyer would declare the cash incentive on the mortgage application form. Most lenders usually do not mind this, provided the valuation carried out by the Lender is in agreement with the selling price.

In this example, each property transaction is carried out completely separately. This means there is no mention of discounts or benefits for buying two or more properties.

In comparing above tables A and B you can see that both parties have benefited. The Seller has been able to find a buyer, sell two (or more) properties, and make a gain of £2,800. (Note: The Buyer could also give the Seller a printed copy of this book and refer to the chapter titled *The Link Strategy For Sellers.)*

Note that in Scenario B (using the strategy) the Buyer comes out better, even though paying £160,000 instead of £150,000 per flat!

What's happening here is that the savings in stamp duty (£3,200 instead of £9,000) are, in effect, being shared by the Buyer and the Seller, so both parties come out winning. The amount 'shared' by each party can be changed by simply changing the selling price or the cash incentive amount.

When buying several properties from a single source, the savings in stamp duty are very significant indeed. In this example, if buying just four flats from the same Seller at £160,000 each, the amount of potential stamp duty *savings* is £19,200! Note: In this example, Peter, the Buyer, is not cheating – he is doing this with a clear conscience because the correct stamp duty is being paid on each and every property transaction, and no multiple transaction has taken place.

Example 8.

Peter buys a flat in a high-rise building for £190,000, plus a parking bay in the basement for £18,000. This is regarded as a linked transaction because both properties are being purchased from the same Seller as part of a single arrangement or series of transactions. It does not matter whether the parking bay is a specific allocated bay or whether you are just buying the right to use any space in the car park. The stamp duty payable is therefore 1% of £208,000.

Alternative Scenario.

Peter buys a flat in a high-rise building for £190,000 and pays stamp duty at 1%. A month (or a year) later, the same Seller contacts Peter and offers him a parking bay that has become available. This is probably not a linked transaction because at the time of buying the flat Peter was not contemplating buying a parking bay and he was not aware that a parking bay was available.

Furthermore, there is no documentary evidence to prove otherwise. Peter decides to accept the Seller's offer, and he buys the parking bay for £18,000. As this is not a linked transaction, Peter pays no stamp duty on the £18,000 because the amount is below the tax threshold of £125,000.

Note that if you are buying property at auction and it is not the first time you have done so, you have to be extremely careful about how you proceed if there is any possibility that you are dealing with the same Seller. Should it be the same Seller, you want to be able to prove (with documentary evidence) that you did *not benefit from* and had *no awareness of* the common ownership. Then, should the tax authorities investigate, you can prove your case.

Another point is that a husband and wife are regarded as linked. You cannot buy one property from the husband and another from his wife as a way of avoiding a linked transaction. The linkage between spouses also extends to immediate family. When it comes to other relatives or work colleagues, the law is vague in terms of what constitutes a 'connected person' so be wary.

To police matters relating to linked transactions, Revenue & Customs has a special department that is informally known as 'COP 10' (coppers come to mind!). COP 10 refers to the Inland Revenue *Code Of Practice* number 10 (a kind of charter). You can see the text of this charter on the internet by going to: *www.hmrc.gov.uk/pdfs/cop10.htm*.

Should the tax authorities suspect possible linkage, the matter would typically be referred to COP 10 for investigation. The COP 10 code of practice explains how they investigate linked transactions and what documents and information would be required in the event of a query.

These documents are:

- Your name and tax reference number;

- Full particulars of the transaction or event in question;

- Copies of all relevant documents with the relevant parts or passages identified;

- Your opinion of the tax consequences of the particular transaction;

- Your explanation of the particular point(s) of difficulty that led to your request;

- Details of what sections of the Taxes Acts you consider to be relevant;

- Particulars of any case law, Inland Revenue extra-statutory concessions or Statements of Practice you consider to be relevant;

- Your reasons for your opinion of the tax consequences of the transaction.

Typically, COP 10 can rule on whether a particular property transaction is to be regarded as linked or not linked for stamp duty purposes. Naturally, if you were to discuss a particular scenario *before* the event, it must be entirely hypothetical. You can hardly claim at a later date that you had no *awareness* if you previously discussed it with COP 10, so tread with caution! COP 10 can be contacted as follows (this address acts for the whole of the UK):

COP 10
Manchester Stamp Office
Upper Fifth Floor
Royal Exchange
Exchange Street
Manchester, M2 7EV

Tel: 0161 834 8109

It is important to know about COP 10 in case you ever have to deal with them. Clearly, if you are dealing with COP 10 you have to remember that you are, in effect, dealing with HM Revenue and Customs.

If the taxman became suspicious about a stamp duty payment it could result in enquiries being made by COP 10. This is what the tax authorities have to say about linked transactions vis-à-vis stamp duty:

"Linked transaction are those which form part of a single scheme, arrangement or series of transactions between the same vendor and purchaser or, in either case, persons connected with them. ICTA88/S839 defines when parties are connected. If a vendor, for example, advertises a house with gardens for sale and the purchase is structured in such a way that the husband buys the house and his wife buys the gardens, these will be regarded as linked transactions.

The rate of tax will be determined by the sum of the chargeable considerations paid for both house and gardens.

It is a question of fact whether or not transactions are linked. A purchaser will need to make a full examination of all the circumstances leading to the transactions before completing their land transaction return. Just because two transactions are between the same purchaser and seller does not necessarily mean they are linked. The transactions will be linked however if they are part of the same deal.

If two transactions are documented separately the form in which the transactions are documented will not determine whether they are linked or not. For example, documenting transactions with separate contracts will not prevent them being linked if the transactions are under arrangements which indicate they are part of a single deal.

Series of transactions means something more than that one transaction following the other. There must be something else to connect the transactions.

It would however be a question of fact whether purchases are totally unrelated. In particular the purchaser needs to consider whether the fact that the first transaction had happened had affected the terms of the second transaction."

(See: www.hmrc.gov.uk/manuals/sdltmanual/SDLTM30100.htm)

This is what it boils down to: whenever you may be buying more than one property from the same Seller (with or without time gaps) make sure that you can pass the *link test* (see Fig. 4).

Note that stamp duty is a self-assessment tax. That is, you the Buyer must decide the correct amount of stamp duty to pay, and you or your solicitor will do this when filling in the stamp duty payment form. Council tax, for example, is not a self-assessment tax because the tax authorities check your home and then tell you exactly how much tax to pay.

In regard to linked transactions, the following questions come to mind:

1. *If I buy a property (either off-plan or ready built) does that mean I can never again buy another property from the same firm without being penalized with extra stamp duty? The answer is YES unless you can pass the link test* (see Fig. 4).

2. *Can I ever buy more than one property from the same Seller without being penalized with extra stamp duty? The answer is NO unless you can pass the link test* (see Fig. 4).

WARNING

According to Revenue and Customs transactions are linked if they form part of an 'arrangement' between the same seller and buyer.

Unfortunately the word 'arrangement' could be interpreted broadly by Revenue. It allows them a lot of flexibility to attack multiple sales between individuals.

However, just because there are multiple sales doesn't necessarily mean they have to be linked. Provided each sale would have taken place irrespective of the other there should be no linkage.

However, even if you believe your transactions are not linked, what matters most is what the tax authorities think.

That's why you should always consult a suitably qualified solicitor or accountant before entering into any purchase where there is a danger of linkage.

Fig. 4 - The Link Test

No awareness: At the time of purchase, you must not be contemplating buying more than one property (from the same Seller). Equally, you must not be aware of any other property purchase made in the past (from the same Seller). This must be backed up with crystal clear *documentary* evidence that is irrefutable.

No benefit: No benefit must be derived from a property purchase as a result of any other property purchase from the same Seller. This must be backed up with crystal clear documentary evidence that is irrefutable.

If there is awareness but no benefit, it will be regarded as a linked transaction unless you can clearly prove with documentary evidence that there was no benefit. Even then, the transaction may be regarded as linked by virtue of awareness alone.

If there was benefit but no awareness, it will be regarded as a linked transaction unless you can clearly prove with documentary evidence that there was no awareness. Even then, the transaction may be regarded as linked by virtue of benefit alone.

If there was no benefit and no awareness it will not be regarded as a linked transaction, but it is still very important to have irrefutable documentary evidence to back this up in case it is queried by the tax authorities.

Section 108 'Linked Transactions' of The Finance Act 2003 is a pointless and pernicious bit of legislation that fully deserves to be abolished. It is pointless because it serves no purpose except to collect more tax from a product that is already taxed. It does not close any so called 'tax loophole' since property transactions that are not linked still get taxed with stamp duty in the usual way. It is pernicious because it serves to castigate bona fide property owners and business people who may buy more than one property from the same Seller. Furthermore, it goes against a fundamental principle of free enterprise: it discourages repeat business and customer loyalty by imposing tax penalties against this.

Using *The Link Strategy* for Selling Property

This strategy can also be used by a *Seller* who may end up selling more than one property to the same Buyer, either as a lot, or as a series of transactions over time. It will also suit anybody selling at auction. The key points to bear in mind if you may be selling more than one property to the same person are as follows:

1. Use the link strategy to help the buyer avoid paying more stamp duty than necessary. You would do this by helping the Buyer avoid the linked property trap as explained in this chapter. Remember that linkage can apply even if selling properties as separate transactions, with time gaps in between.

2. Use this strategy to build repeat business and customer loyalty with property investors. You would do this by helping the Buyer avoid the linked property trap, as explained above.

3. Offer property *free of stamp duty.* You would do this without incurring financial loss, as a way of generating greater buyer interest, and as a means of securing a successful sale. Do this by building the cost of stamp duty into the selling price, by using Cash Incentives, and by helping Buyers avoid the linked property trap.

4. Remember that a husband and wife (and close relatives) are regarded as 'connected' and if selling property through both, it will be regarded as a linked transaction.

5. Study the examples given in this chapter to understand how best to help repeat Buyers avoid a linked transaction trap.

6. If you are planning to sell more than one property to the same buyer and you want to get clarification from the tax authorities so as to avoid linkage before proceeding, be very careful! By discussing the deal with the tax authorities you may no longer be able to help a potential Buyer pass the *link test* for awareness.

7. If there is any possibility that you will be selling more than one property to the same Buyer (now or in the future), make sure that you will be able to help the Buyer pass the *link test* by studying this chapter and planning your sales strategy carefully.

Summary of *The Link Strategy:*

1. Use this strategy to avoid paying additional stamp duty when buying more than one property from the same Seller (with or without time gaps).

2. Remember that a husband and wife are regarded as 'connected' and if buying property from both, it will be regarded as a linked transaction.

3. Study the examples given in this chapter to understand how not to fall into a linked transaction trap.

4. If you are planning a property deal that could be regarded as a linked transaction and you want to get clarification from the tax authorities before proceeding, be very careful! By discussing the deal with the tax authorities you may no longer be able to pass the *link test* for awareness for that particular deal.

5. If there is any possibility that you will be buying more than one property from the same Seller (now or in the future), make sure that you will be able to pass the *link test* by studying this chapter and planning your strategy carefully.

6. If you are *selling* more than one property to the same person use the link strategy to reduce the amount of stamp duty paid by the Buyer. By doing this both the Seller and the Buyer will benefit financially.

The Mortgage Cashback Strategy

When considering a mortgage you will be presented with many options, such as fixed or variable interest, the rate of interest, with or without redemption penalties, interest only or capital repayment, and so on.

There is a bewildering range of mortgages from many different financial institutions, adding up to many possibilities for borrowing money. Before you start to look for a mortgage, your requirements need to be carefully worked out. Below is a simple check list to go through, to establish the kind of mortgage you might need (see Fig. 5).

Fig. 5 is not a complete list of all the mortgage options available in the UK. But it is a useful check list: consider each item as it best applies to you and begin to narrow down the kind of mortgage you may need. You must get a rough idea about the kind of mortgage you can apply for *before* you start hunting for a property to buy. Once you have found a property you will then be able to negotiate a better price knowing what kind of mortgage you are likely to get.

The Mortgage Cashback Strategy involves getting a mortgage that gives a cashback (i.e. a lump sum of money) that can be used towards your property purchase costs or anything else. Note that the cashback comes from the Lender, not from the Seller.

For a good general introduction to the mortgage scene in the UK go to the Motley Fool website at:

www.fool.co.uk/mortgages/articles/mortgagebasics.htm

This is what they have to say about cashbacks:

> *"Some of the instant inducements include the offer of a lump sum in cash once the forms are signed. The 'cashback', as it's called, can obviously be useful if you haven't got any spare money to pay for furniture or legal fees or moving costs. However, as always, watch out for the small print. Some providers reserve the right to claim part of this money back if you switch mortgages within a certain timescale."*

Fig. 5 - Mortgage Check List

'Comments' column shows issues to be considered to narrow down the kind of mortgage required

Item	Mortgage feature	Comments
1	Buy-to-let mortgage	Rental income needs to cover mortgage repayments
2	Own home mortgage	Will you be living there?
3	Interest only	Best for buy-to-let
4	Capital repayment	Best for own home mortgage
5	Fixed interest rate	Do you think interest rates will go up or down in the years to come?
6	Variable interest rate (also known as 'Standard Variable Rate')	Best if planning to sell soon. This is the best kind of mortgage to apply for if you want a mortgage cashback.
7	Deposit amount	e.g. 15% deposit paid by Buyer
8	No deposit	i.e. 100% mortgage
9	With redemption penalties?	Will the lender penalize you if the mortgage is repaid or remortgaged? Typically, redemption penalties apply for the first one to three years of mortgage. So if not planning to sell in short term, redemption penalties may not matter.
10	Self certification	Can you prove you are earning a salary? If not, or if self-employed, apply for a self certification mortgage.
11	Cashback	You get a cashback (i.e. a sum of money) given to you by the lender in addition to the loan for the property. Cashbacks typically range from £500 to £5,000 or more.

Cashback deals are usually available only on loans with standard variable rates. As many Lenders in the UK offer mortgage cashbacks you should take full advantage provided the redemption penalties are acceptable. To find out the kind of cashback you can get, proceed as follows:

1. Go to a mortgage broker who will not charge for his services. Most mortgage brokers are free because they get paid commission by the Lender when they arrange a mortgage. Since they get commission from just about all Lenders, they can afford to be impartial in their advice to you.

2. See a broker *before* you have found a property to buy, so that you can get the mortgage set up in advance. Endeavour to fill in any forms as far as possible, to determine the kind of mortgage you might need (this will save time later when getting the mortgage).

3. Tell the broker that you want a mortgage to buy a property (explain why you want to buy a property, is it buy-to-let, will you be re-selling, how much deposit will you be paying, and so on). Ask the broker to show you some good examples of the kind of mortgage that would suit you.

4. Tell the broker you are interested in cashback mortgages and see what can be offered. You may find that a good cashback mortgage goes hand-in-hand with a not-so-good interest rate, or a not-so-good redemption penalty (it's swings and roundabouts). But interest rates may not matter that much if you are planning to re-sell soon. Equally, redemption penalties may not matter if you are planning to keep the property for several years without remortgaging. The point is this: go for as big a cashback as you can get if the other factors in the mortgage deal are acceptable.

TIP

You can save thousands of pounds over the term of a mortgage by not buying 'buildings insurance' through your mortgage lender. You are not obliged to get insurance from the same lender that is giving you a mortgage, or even from a company recommended by your Lender. Smaller insurance companies tend to give better insurance deals compared with the large 'High Street' lenders.

Some mortgage brokers will be able to find deals that offer up to 7.5% mortgage cashback – this can amount to £15,000 or £20,000! Beware the small print, as there may be stiff 'penalties' in terms of redemption penalties, interest rates, deposit requirements and so on. A good way to gauge a cashback mortgage is to get the details of a good mortgage deal that meets your requirements *without* any cashback. Then use this as a template for comparing mortgage deals that offer cashbacks.

A redemption penalty is the main 'sting in the tail' applied to mortgage cashback offers. The term 'redemption penalty' refers to the cost you will have to pay the Lender if you decide to pay off your mortgage or switch to another mortgage company.

Redemption penalties are usually for a fixed term, e.g. three years, and then disappear.

Do not be put off by redemption penalties. They can be perfectly acceptable if, for instance, you are buying a home and you have no plans to remortgage or move home again in the near future. Provided you understand and accept the terms of the redemption penalty (and other aspects of the mortgage), it makes sense to go for the biggest mortgage cashback you can get.

Some Lenders offer cashbacks in the form of 'free gifts' – a growing trend in the UK. For example, West Bromwich Building Society made headlines by offering a free Rover car instead of a cashback (with a redemption penalty that lasted five years).

Also, consider the alternative of getting a *remortgage cashback*. In this scenario, you would remortgage your home or some other property that you already own, get a cashback, and use the remortgage money to purchase a property for cash.

Although we are talking about getting cashbacks from *Lenders*, you can sometimes get small cashbacks from *mortgage brokers*: Once you've decided on a mortgage product it is worth considering purchasing it through a mortgage broker. As UK mortgage brokers receive commission for selling financial products, they will often split this money with you if asked. You can often get a cashback in the region of £100-£300.

But remember that mortgage brokers may not actually be able to offer the product you are looking for, so carefully consider alternatives offered. Don't be put off if the brokers can't provide what you have decided upon: carry on phoning around, or even get in touch with the mortgage company directly and ask them which brokers supply their mortgages.

TIP

If researching on the internet, do not be tempted to fill in mortgage application forms online. Why? Because, every time you fill in a mortgage application form online (or even request a quotation online) the Lender or broker will automatically do a credit check on you. And every time a credit check is done it counts as a black mark on your credit rating (the fewer credit checks that go into your records the better).

To get an idea of what is available in the way of cashback mortgages, check it out on the internet. Simply enter 'cashback mortgage' in Google UK, tick the 'pages from the UK' option and you will get many responses and offers. Other ways to get mortgage cashback information:

1. Check the local property newspapers for mortgage company and broker advertisements.

2. Check the national newspapers (every national newspaper has a particular day of the week when they focus on property and mortgage advertisements – usually a Friday or Saturday).

3. Buy a mortgage magazine from any good magazine retailer. These are full of advice and mortgage offers that include cashbacks.

Most of the big mortgage companies offer basic mortgage cashbacks. A typical offer will be for a £500 cashback, to be repaid over three years. Other cashbacks have no repayment requirements, and amount to 'gifts'.

Summary of *The Mortgage Cashback Strategy:*

1. Go for a cashback if the mortgage deal as a whole is acceptable, and use the cashback money to pay for stamp duty and other conveyancing costs.

2. Go for the largest cashback offer available, all things being equal.

3. Use a free mortgage broker to make a shortlist of two or three possible mortgage cashbacks suitable to your requirements. Also, check mortgage magazines.

4. Do as much form filling as possible with the mortgage broker so that when the mortgage application is made for a particular property, time is saved. When you visit the broker *for the first time* take your passport and a utility bill (this will save time at a later stage).

5. Keep an eye on the mortgage market by using the internet, property newspapers, and magazines.

The Price Strategy

This is a great strategy for saving stamp duty costs and it applies to most situations involved in buying residential property. Normally, when a property price is agreed between Buyer and Seller, this is the figure that goes on your mortgage application form. Provided the valuation carried out by the Lender is not *less* than the agreed property price, the Buyer will usually get a mortgage based upon this figure.

To explain further we will look at the following example:

Example

- Seller's asking price: £210,000.

- The rock bottom amount that the Seller is willing to accept: £200,000.

- Buyer only wants to pay £190,000, so there is a price gap of £10,000.

- Buyer can get a 95% Loan To Value mortgage.

- Deposit is therefore 5%.

In this example there is an impasse over the price. This is a common occurrence as Sellers often get offers below their asking price. If the Buyer and Seller cannot find common ground, the deal is lost and no sale goes ahead. But using *The Price Strategy* this needn't be the case. We will compare two scenarios based on this example:

Scenario one, based on the traditional approach

- Asking price: £210,000

- Discounted amount (price after negotiation): £200,000.

- Mortgage amount is £190,000 (95% of £200,000).

- Mortgage Deposit (payment from Buyer to Buyer's Lender): £10,000 (5% of £200,000).

- Buyer has to pay stamp duty, legal fees, mortgage valuation, and all other costs out of his own resources as these cannot be included in the mortgage or property bank loan.

- Property would be registered at the land registry with a value of £200,000.

- Deal goes ahead if Buyer agrees a selling price of £200,000 and has enough savings to pay for the mortgage deposit, stamp duty, and all other conveyancing costs. In this scenario the deal is lost as the Buyer wants a price of £190,000.

 ## *Scenario two based on The Price Strategy*

- Asking price: £210,000

- Discounted amount (price agreed after negotiation): £200,000.

- Cash Incentive agreed (payment from Seller to Buyer): £10,000 (difference between £210,000 and £200,000, so Seller ends up getting £200,000 for house).

- Mortgage amount is £199,500 (95% of £210,000).

- Mortgage Deposit (payment from Buyer to Buyer's Lender): £10,500 (5% of £210,000).

- Buyer can pay for stamp duty, legal fees, mortgage valuation, and all other costs from the £10,000 cash incentive, and still have money left over.

- Property would be registered at the land registry with a value of £210,000.

- Deal goes ahead, based on a selling price of £210,000 because the Buyer has a cash incentive of £10,000 which greatly helps pay for the mortgage deposit, stamp duty, and all other conveyancing costs.

We will now look at scenario two in more detail and explain the strategy further. What follows is a step-by-step procedure, including suggested dialogue.

STEP 1: Negotiate a price.

STEP 2: Make an offer.

STEP 3: Confirm it in writing.

STEP 1: Negotiate a price.

- The Buyer will naturally negotiate the best price he can, and here we assume the price has been negotiated down to £200,000 in the 'conventional' manner. Hence, a £10,000 price reduction has been achieved (most Sellers will agree to reduce the price to some degree if they think they have found a buyer – it's just a matter of finding out the lowest price that the Seller is willing to come down to).

- Whether or not the Seller is willing to reduce the price, *The Price Strategy* can be used to good effect. In any event, STEP 1 involves getting the best price you can *before* starting to use *The Price Strategy*.

STEP 2: Make an offer.

You go on to this step only after one of the following has occurred:

- You have negotiated the best price you can get and a price reduction has been agreed in principle.

- You have negotiated the best price you can get and no price reduction was possible.

In this example we will assume that a price reduction from £210,000 to £200,000 is on offer from the Seller. Later we will cover a situation where no price reduction is available. You now start to apply the strategy.

You start by confirming the price reduction that has been agreed. You then go on to ask the Seller to agree the asking price of £210,000! This apparent *volte-face* may come as a surprise to the Seller, but the Buyer goes on to explain that the price to be paid will still only be £200,000. The dialogue would go along the lines that follow.

Note: Speak slowly when negotiating, don't rush things through. Also, pause after each 'chunk' of dialogue to make sure the Seller has heard you correctly, and make certain there are no misunderstandings. If you get any questions and you don't want to stop at that point, say *'I will go on to explain that in just a moment'*.

Dialogue:

- *'Now that we've agreed a price of £200,000, this is the amount I will be paying you. I like your house very much, and it shouldn't be devalued. I want to enter the full market value (in other words, the full asking price) on the Land Registry. Therefore I want to ask you to agree a selling price of £210,000. I also want to ask you to give me a Cash Incentive of £10,000. So you get paid £210,000, and you give me back £10,000. This means you will still be getting the agreed £200,000, but the house value will go through on the Land Registry as £210,000.'*

- *'The house price of £210,000 is the price that would go on all the paperwork including my mortgage application. The Cash Incentive of £10,000 will help me pay for legal fees, stamp duty and other costs, and in carrying out certain renovation work before I move in.'*

- *'This method of buying your house won't affect you in any way. On completion, my solicitor will give your solicitor the agreed selling price of £210,000. Your solicitor will then give my solicitor the agreed £10,000 Cash Incentive. Of course, you will need to tell your solicitor about this and I'll give you a letter for your solicitor which explains all this.'*

- *'All that we have discussed is completely legal and above board, and is common practice throughout the building industry. The £10,000 price difference is a cash incentive, and any experienced conveyancer will be familiar with this way of doing business. This £10,000 is a cash incentive from you to me but the money does not come from you – it comes from the money I am borrowing to buy your house.'*

- *'The cash incentive is, in effect, a payment from my Lender to me, but it goes through your solicitor. The following diagram shows how this works.'*

(See the diagram in Fig. 6 on the next page – give the Seller a copy, and go through it together).

To finish this point, explain that the cash incentive amounts to surplus money that is left over (the difference between the amount borrowed and the amount actually paid for the property). You now continue the dialogue to finish the negotiations.

- *'Have a look at these advertisements. What I am proposing is no different to the way large building companies operate. You and I are doing the same thing but on a smaller scale. In these advertisements, the building companies are selling directly to buyers, just as you are selling directly to me.'*

(Show advertisements depicting cash incentive offers from builders like Barratt. Answer any remaining questions).

- *'If you can help me out by doing this I will be very pleased to buy your (fridge/curtains/sofa/flower pots/whatever) for £300. I will pay you cash for these items in a separate transaction. So you will end up getting the £200,000 payment for the house, and in addition you get a separate cash payment direct from me for £300.'*

Make sure that you have established beforehand in your own mind which item (or items) you will be buying for £300. It needs to be an item of little value, or an item that would have been included in the price of the house anyway. That way, the £300 will be genuinely appreciated.

Fig. 6 - Money-flow Diagram

Step 1
LENDER (money loaned to Buyer, based on selling price)

Step 2
BUYER'S SOLICITOR (Money given to Buyer's solicitor for buying property)

Step 3
SELLER'S SOLICITOR (Money paid to Seller's solicitor on completion, without deducting the cash incentive)

Step 4
BUYER'S SOLICITOR (Seller's solicitor 'pays' cash incentive money to Buyer's solicitor for giving to Buyer)

Step 5
BUYER Buyer receives cash incentive money as part of the final reconciliation of the completion statement prepared by Buyer's solicitor

- *'If you will agree to this method of selling your property this is how you will benefit:*

  1. *'You get to sell your property at the agreed price.*

  2. *'You can stop looking for a buyer as you will now be able to sell your property. It means you can move on with other things in your life, knowing that you have sold this house.*

  3. *'Your property will not be devalued in the local market place as it will be registered at the higher value of £210,000. This can benefit you or your relatives who may own other properties in the area.*

  4. *'You get an additional £300 as a separate cash payment direct from me.'*

(Give the Seller a separate sheet showing these four benefits.)

- *'So can I take it that you agree in principle with this strategy? If so, I will give you a letter confirming my agreement to buy your house. I will also give you a letter that you can send to your solicitor which explains the strategy we have been talking about.'*

  Stop to make sure the Seller has heard you correctly, and make certain there are no misunderstandings. At this point you must wait to get an answer to know whether or not the Seller is going to co-operate. Do not proceed to STEP 3, if it is clear that the Seller will not co-operate.

Summary of the Seller benefits:

1. Seller has found a Buyer and can sell the house.

2. Seller gets to sell the house at the desired price.

3. Seller's house is not devalued in the local market place (this can benefit the Seller if he/she owns other local properties, or has nearby relatives who own properties).

4. Seller gets an additional payment (£300 in this example) for co-operating with the strategy.

Summary of the Buyer benefits:

1. Buyer gets to buy the property at a bargain price because, as a result of getting the cash incentive, he paid much less than the registered price.

2. Buyer gets a property with instant equity.

3. Buyer gets cash (in this example £10,000) that can be used to pay for stamp duty, legal fees, conveyancing costs, or just be put into a savings account!

TIP

Prepare a sheet of paper that just shows the four Seller benefits mentioned above. Use a large size font and use the word 'you' instead of 'Seller'. Give this sheet to the Seller when you mention the benefits.

The key to *The Price Strategy* is the price difference between the 'official' price on which the mortgage is based and the actual amount paid to the Seller. This difference is the *cash incentive*. In the building industry it is common for house builders to offer cash incentives, and the amount of the cash incentive will have been factored into the selling price. Hence, there is no legal difference between a cash incentive offered by a house builder and a cash incentive offered by a private individual as described in this strategy.

Ideally the cash incentive should not be more than 5% to 10% of the PRICE. If it is not over 5% (as in this example) it is more likely to be accepted by most Lenders. Note that cash incentives of 15% or more are not uncommon in the building industry.

Note: The Buyer should always declare the *cash incentive* on his mortgage application form (there is nothing to hide). Most Lenders will usually not mind that the Buyer is getting a cash incentive provided the selling price is in line with the valuation report. Remember three things: (i) The *Cash Incentive* is not an additional loan from the Lender, (ii) the Lender is not involved with the cash incentive in any direct or legal sense, and (iii) Lenders themselves give cash incentives to Buyers (just look at any mortgage magazine).

However, it's important to note that some Lenders do not accept private vendor cash incentives so speak to a good mortgage broker before you take any action.

A cash incentive received by a Buyer is not usually regarded as income and should therefore be tax free. This is so because the amount is relatively small. The cashback is akin to a gift – if you receive a gift of money it is tax free, like winning the lottery!

However, if you are in the business of buying and selling property for a living, then the *Cash Incentive* could be regarded as income or profit and taxed, just like any other earned income. Advice from a tax accountant may be appropriate.

Regarding Capital Gains Tax, this will not apply if buying or selling your own home (the place where you live). If the property is bought or sold by a property investor it gets a bit more complicated:

Buyer. If a property is bought at a higher price by virtue of getting a cash incentive, the Buyer who is a property investor will possibly pay *less* capital gains tax if and when selling because the price *difference* will be that much less. However, it is possible that the taxman could base the CGT calculation on the lower price (net of the cash incentive) if this is regarded as a better approximation of the property's market value.

Seller. If a property is sold at a higher price by virtue of agreeing to a cash incentive, the Seller who is a property investor may end up paying *more* capital gains tax if and when selling because the price *difference* will be that much more. Hence, the *Cash Incentive* may ultimately have the effect of increasing the capital gains tax bill, assuming the Seller is liable for capital gains tax anyway. There are many ways to avoid or mitigate capital gains tax and therefore a Cash Incentive may have little or no effect. But remember that capital gains tax is not applicable if buying or selling your own home.

54

Important clarification regarding '*gifted deposits*':

- Do not confuse a *Cash Incentive*, as described in this book, with a so called '*gifted deposit*'. Nothing in this book makes use of a *gifted deposit*. In the past, *gifted deposits* were used as a means of getting an amount of money from a Lender that was *higher* than the selling price of the property. However, most Lenders no longer offer 'gifted deposit mortgages'.

- The strategies given in this book do not involve *gifted deposits*. Instead, a cash incentive is obtained from the Seller, a transaction that does not involve the Lender. Cash Incentives of this kind are widely used by house-building companies.

- A *Cash Incentive* is fundamentally different to a *gifted deposit* because (i) the lender is not involved in the cash incentive transaction, and (ii) the mortgage amount is based on the selling price only (with a *gifted deposit* the mortgage amount is based on the sum of the selling price PLUS the *gifted deposit* amount). A Lender is involved with a gifted deposit because the money for the gifted deposit is paid by the Lender to the Buyer, via the solicitor. It is important to make sure your solicitor understands the difference, and that you are not proposing to get involved with any kind of *gifted deposit*.

- Lenders are phasing out *gifted deposits* (even though they are legal) because 'mission creep' has set in. That is, the amount of the *gifted deposit* requested by borrowers (in addition to the loan amount to buy the property) was going up to 15%, 20%, and even 25% of the property value. As a result, some Buyers ended up taking on mortgage debts that they could not afford to repay. The tabloid press had a field day blaming Lenders for lending too much money to 'vulnerable' people.

- The *Cash Incentive* strategies proposed in this book are different because the Lenders are not involved in the process. The *Cash Incentive* is a private arrangement between the Buyer and the Seller (albeit through solicitors), and provided the mortgage is based on the SELLING PRICE and VALUATION, it is likely to be acceptable to many Lenders.

To reassure the Seller about this way of doing business, explain that virtually all house building companies operate this way. Show the Seller some typical advertisements, such as:

A. Advertisement extract from Kingsoak Homes: *'Options include 5% deposit paid, up to £10,000 cashback, stamp duty paid, home exchange, investor package.'*

B. Advertisement extract from Barratt Homes: *'Purchase plans include home exchange, 5% deposit paid, stamp duty paid, £5,000 cashback, investor package.'*

An examination of the Barratt's advertisement shows the following: Barratt is the Seller. So when a house is bought from Barratt, you the Buyer get a sum of money, i.e. a cash incentive. In this example, the cash incentive takes the form of a 5% deposit payment, a stamp duty payment, £5,000 in cash, and so on. In other words, Barratt is giving the Buyer a sum of money (financial package) as a reward for buying its property.

Note that Barratt has factored the cost of the cash incentive into its selling price, and that the Buyer will be getting a mortgage based on this selling price.

The Price Strategy uses the same strategy employed by Barratt and many other property builders. In the example at the beginning of this chapter, the Seller is giving you, the Buyer, a £10,000 cash incentive in return for buying their property.

Thus when you apply *The Price Strategy* you are, in effect, enabling the Seller to use the same selling methods used by large national builders. There is absolutely nothing underhand about this strategy – it is perfectly legal and proper. Private individuals have the same right to use this strategy as much as house-building companies do. So when you go to meet a Seller to negotiate a price, go equipped with advertisements from builders such as Barratt and Kingsoak.

Note that if using a Cash Incentive to finance a mortgage deposit, a Buyer may have to obtain a bridging loan for two or three days (the time interval between paying the deposit to the solicitor to complete the deal and receiving the cash incentive to repay the bridging loan).

Make sure that you brief your solicitor about your intentions to ask for a 'cash incentive' in your negotiations, should this be necessary. Do this *before* you start to look for a property to buy. If your solicitor is not familiar with the concept of a cash incentive in a property transaction you should perhaps find another solicitor. Then, if a Seller needs reassurance about the strategy, you can tell the Seller to ask his solicitor to contact your solicitor to get confirmation that a *Cash Incentive* is a perfectly acceptable way of proceeding.

STEP 3: Confirm it in writing.

Let's recap. In step 1 you negotiated the best possible price without using any of the strategies in this book. In step 2 you made an offer based on *The Price Strategy* and you got a positive response indicating co-operation with the strategy. Now, in step 3 you will be giving the Seller two letters.

The first letter is a written confirmation from you to the Seller to clarify the offer you have just made. This first letter would be issued in duplicate so that the Seller can sign and return one copy to you to indicate an agreement in principle to proceed.

The second letter is a draft letter for the Seller to send to his solicitor to get things moving. Both these letters are shown below, with suggested wording that can be adapted as necessary.

Note: these two letters would also be copied to any estate agent that may be involved in the transaction.

Written confirmation of offer from Buyer to Seller

(date)

From: (Buyer's name and address)

To: (Seller's name and address)

Re: Sale of your property *(enter property address)*

Following my viewing of your property, I would like to make a formal offer at the full asking price, made up as follows:

Full Offer Price:	*£ (enter agreed price)* *[Note: In the case of the above example, this would be £210,000]*
*Less Cash Incentive: **(For redecoration, repairs, and miscellaneous costs)**	*£ (enter agreed amount)* *[Note: In the case of the above example, this would be £10,000]*
Total cash on completion:	*£ (enter difference of above two figures)* *[Note: In the case of the above example, this would be £200,000]*

* The Cash Incentive referred to above is a sum of money that will be paid from the Seller's solicitor to the Buyer's solicitor on completion of the property transaction.

The address of my solicitor is as follows: (enter Buyer's solicitor details).

I confirm that I will declare the cash incentive on my mortgage application form. (Delete this paragraph if Buyer is not using a loan to buy the property.)

This offer remains subject to satisfactory valuation and contract. The next step is to tell your solicitor to sell your property to me as explained above.

If an estate agent is involved, you need to ask the estate agent to issue a 'memorandum of sale' and withdraw the property from the market. ***Please ensure that your estate agent clearly understands that the SELLING PRICE is the higher amount (before deduction of the Cash Incentive).*** *No discount applies to this transaction and the word 'discount' should not appear on any documentation as this would be incorrect. When I receive a copy of the memorandum of sale I will ask my Lender to carry out the mortgage valuation on the property.*

Please sign the declaration below and give me a copy of this letter to indicate that you agree in principle to sell me your house on the terms given above.

If anything is not clear please contact me at any time.

Yours sincerely,

(enter Buyer's name)

DECLARATION BY SELLER: *I agree in principle to sell you my property on the terms described above, subject to valuation and subject to contract.*

Signed: ………………………………….. *Date:*………..

Print Name: ………………………………………….

Letter from Seller to Seller's solicitor

Dear (Solicitor)

Property: *(Address)*

I have asked you to act for me in the selling of my above property. I am writing to explain that I have found a buyer and the details are as follows:

1. *Name of buyer: (enter name).*

2. *Buyer's solicitor: (enter name, address, and telephone number).*

3. *Price for selling property: (enter SELLING PRICE, not discounted amount).*

4. *Cash Incentive: I have also agreed to give the buyer a Cash Incentive of £ (enter amount). This sum of money is to be paid to the buyer or his solicitor upon completion, from the proceeds of sale. This means that the total cash on completion will be £xyz (the agreed price of £..... less the Cash Incentive of £.....).*

   The Buyer will be declaring this Cash Incentive on his mortgage application form. (Delete this paragraph if the buyer is not borrowing money to buy the property.)

Please find enclosed a copy of the offer I have received from the buyer.

Yours sincerely

(name of Seller)

The second letter, from the Seller to his solicitor, is important as it will focus the Seller's mind into taking the correct action and being committed to following the strategy.

If the Seller will not sign the declaration in the letter there and then, you should allow the Seller to take the letter away, and consult a solicitor should they wish to. In this event, you should make it clear that you cannot commit to buying the property (and you will be looking at other properties) until the letter is signed or until you get a clear indication of an intention to sell the property to you.

Important Note: *When mentioning this strategy to a solicitor, only talk in terms of getting a Cash Incentive from the Seller. Do not talk in terms of getting a cashback from the Lender as this is not the case, and solicitors may regard this as somewhat dubious. Also, point out that you will be declaring the cash incentive on the mortgage application form, and that this is no different to getting a Cash Incentive from a house-building company, a practice that is common all over the UK.*

In effect, *The Price Strategy* uses the *Lender's money* rather than your own money (assuming you have any!) to pay for stamp duty and other costs. In the above example it is much better to end up with a mortgage of £199,500 and have £10,000 cash-in-hand, than to end up with a mortgage of £190,000 and *no* cash-in-hand.

You may end up paying a little more in monthly interest on a mortgage of £199,500 compared with £190,000, but this difference is small. For example, if the mortgage interest is 5%, the monthly payment would be about £831 compared to £792 (a difference of about £39). Remember, you don't have to spend all of the Cash Incentive – you can if you wish, put some of the Cash Incentive money into a high-interest savings account to offset the small increase in monthly interest.

Or you could use any money remaining from the Cash Incentive to reduce your mortgage. You can even factor the Cash Incentive into the mortgage deposit, thereby reducing the amount you have to pay as a deposit. Another advantage is that you have £10,000 cash-in-hand (in this example) at a time when you most need it.

But the main advantage is that the £10,000 Cash Incentive has enabled the Buyer (in this example) to secure a house instead of losing it.

When buying your home with limited savings and limited income, a Cash Incentive can sometimes make or break a property deal. Remember: this is a *Cash Incentive* even though the money originates from the mortgage/loan money. If your <u>mortgage</u> also includes a Cash Incentive this is a *mortgage cashback*, which is quite a different animal (see *The Mortgage Cashback Strategy* in another chapter). Of course, there is nothing to stop you getting two cashbacks in the same deal: One from the Seller, and one from the Lender.

If you are running a buy-to-let business, *The Price Strategy* will improve your cash flow and give you more equity. And the small increase in monthly interest will not matter as much since it should be allowed as a tax deduction.

No Price Reduction

We have seen that the amount of the Cash Incentive relates directly to the amount of the price reduction that can be negotiated. In our example the price reduction was £10,000 and hence the Cash Incentive was £10,000. But what happens when no price reduction is available?

In this scenario, the Buyer must decide whether he still wants to buy the property even though the Seller will not agree to any price reduction. If so, *The Price Strategy* can still be used to good effect and this is how it works.

- The objective is to buy the property without having to pay for stamp duty out of your own resources. The solution is to get the Lender (the mortgage company) to pay for the stamp duty. But Lenders will not do this because they normally only lend money for the cost of the actual property.

- The way round this is to ask the Seller to increase the SELLING PRICE by an amount equivalent to (or a bit more than) the stamp duty, rounded off to the nearest one hundred pounds. The Buyer would then get a mortgage based on this higher price.

- For example, if the asking price is £210,000 and no price reduction is possible, the Buyer would ask the Seller to increase the price to, say, £213,000. This would be the agreed SELLING PRICE on *all* relevant documents.

- The Buyer would also ask the Seller for a £3,000 Cash Incentive, using the same negotiating strategy described in this chapter. The net result is that the Seller gets the asking price of £210,000, and the Buyer gets a mortgage based on £213,000 plus £3,000 cash in hand.

- Note that in the negotiating strategy described in this chapter it is suggested that the Buyer give the Seller £300 by buying some chattels. However, the amount of £300 is not set in stone; this could, for example, be reduced to £100.

- This strategy is perfectly legal and proper since the tax authorities will be getting even more stamp duty than otherwise. Furthermore, nobody has been misled, and provided the mortgage valuation is not lower than the SELLING PRICE of £213,000 the Lender will be happy.

Note that you can combine both scenarios: if you get a small price reduction of, say, £500, you could ask for a Cash Incentive of £3,500 (the difference between the SELLING PRICE of £213,000 and the £209,500 to be paid for the property). In this scenario, each party would tell their solicitors that the SELLING PRICE is £213,000 and the Cash Incentive is £3,500.

In fact, in most property transactions it will be a matter of combining two amounts and getting a Cash Incentive for the total. These two amounts will be: (i) the difference between the asking price and the reduced price negotiated, and (ii) the difference between the asking price and a higher price based on adding the stamp duty.

To clarify this further, here is an example:

Example

1. The asking price is £210,000.

2. **Discount amount £5,000.** After negotiation a price reduction of £5,000 is on offer, bringing the price down to £205,000.

3. **Stamp duty amount £2,000.** The stamp duty on £210,000 at 1% is £2,100, so the Seller is asked to increase the selling price by, say £2,000 (from £210,000 to £212,000).

4. The Seller is asked for a Cash Incentive of £7,000 (the total of the discount amount of £5,000 and the stamp duty amount of £2,000).

5. The Seller gets paid the agreed £205,000 and the Buyer gets a mortgage based on £212,000 with a Cash Incentive of £7,000.

When the two elements (the discount amount and the stamp duty amount) are combined, this is a very powerful and effective strategy.

Using the Price Strategy for Selling Property

This strategy will enable a Seller to:

- Offer a property free of stamp duty as a means of attracting interest.

- Get a higher selling price than otherwise.

- Resolve a price impasse, whenever a Seller and Buyer cannot agree a price. Think of the strategy as a way of 'bridging the price gap' whenever a price cannot be agreed.

A Seller would only use this strategy when:

1. The Buyer and Seller cannot agree a price, or when a Buyer cannot pay the amount wanted by the Seller (for whatever reason).

2. The Buyer is willing to agree a price but cannot afford the mortgage deposit or the buying costs (stamp duty, legal fees, etc).

As already mentioned, when a PRICE is agreed between Buyer and Seller, this is the figure that goes on the Buyer's mortgage application form. And provided that the valuation carried out by the Lender is not *less* than the PRICE, the Buyer will usually get a mortgage based on this figure. To be clear on this important point: **the loan amount is based on the PRICE provided the VALUATION is not lower than the PRICE.**

The *Price Strategy* can be used effectively by a Seller by helping the Buyer get a mortgage based on a *higher* price than the amount to be paid to the Seller for the property. That way, the buyer ends up with 'cash in hand'.

To explain further we will look at the following example:

Example

- Seller's asking price: £210,000 and free of stamp duty.

- Rock bottom amount that Seller is willing to accept: £200,000, but not free of stamp duty.

- Maximum amount that Buyer is willing to pay: £197,000.

- Assumption: Buyer can get a 95% Loan To Value mortgage.

- Deposit is therefore 5%.

Looking at the first aspect of this example, let's consider whether the Seller should offer a property 'free of stamp duty'. Clearly, in doing so, the Seller is undertaking to pay the stamp duty 'on behalf' of the Buyer. To compensate, the Seller can simply increase the selling price by the amount of the stamp duty applicable. Many house-building companies do this. For example, in its advertisements, *Berkeley Homes* offers properties by stating 'Stamp Duty Paid'. There is absolutely no reason why a private Seller cannot do the same, and indeed estate agents are happy to be instructed to do this.

Remember, however, that some Lenders will not accept private vendor cash incentives. It is imperative that the Buyer is aware of this fact and speaks to a suitably qualified mortgage broker.

Here are the advantages and disadvantages of offering a property free of stamp duty:

Advantages:

1. Seller gets more market interest because the offer is perceived to be more attractive.

2. Seller can set a price that is close to the stamp duty threshold (e.g. £255,000) without meeting buyer resistance.

3. Seller has greater room for negotiation because the price can be lowered subject to the stamp duty being paid by the Buyer.

4. Seller is able to include the cost of stamp duty in the Buyer's mortgage, thus giving the Buyer another reason for buying the property. This is so because if the price has been increased to take into account the cost of stamp duty, the mortgage will be based on the increased price.

5. Seller has a great bargaining tool: *'If you buy my house you won't have to pay stamp duty.'*

Disadvantages:

1. Seller may meet market resistance to a higher property price that includes the cost of stamp duty.

2. Seller may not be able to offer a competitive price compared to other similar properties being sold nearby.

3. Some Buyers may regard it as a 'sales gimmick' of no significance. Note, however, that this would be wrong. If a Buyer is using a mortgage facility, the mortgage or bank loan will not normally include stamp duty. When the price has the stamp duty factored in, the mortgage will include the cost of the stamp duty.

Note that when the Seller pays stamp duty, it *must be* paid through the Buyer as only the Buyer (or his solicitor) can sign the stamp duty payment form. So in practice, the Seller would give the stamp duty money to the buyer (either directly or through solicitors) for passing on to the tax authorities.

Should you on balance offer the property free of stamp duty and factor this into the selling price? The answer is generally YES provided that you are not in a *price* competition with a similar property being sold next door. You can, of course, factor in just part of the cost of stamp duty, and round off the selling price to the nearest one thousand pounds.

From now onwards you can always sell a property by offering: 'stamp duty paid'. You can either increase the price to compensate for the cost, absorb the cost yourself, or go half and half.

Coming back to our example above, we see that there is an impasse: a price cannot be agreed. This is a common occurrence as Sellers often get offers below their asking price. If the Buyer and Seller cannot find common ground, the deal is lost and no sale goes ahead. But using *The Price Strategy* this needn't be the case. We will now compare two scenarios based on this example:

Scenario one, based on the conventional approach

1. Asking price: £210,000 with no stamp duty to pay (i.e. the Seller pays the stamp duty).

2. Maximum price reduction Seller is willing to go to: £200,000, but Buyer pays stamp duty.

3. Mortgage amount for Buyer would be £190,000 (95% of £200,000).

4. Mortgage Deposit (payment from Buyer to Buyer's Lender) would be: £10,000 (5% of £200,000).

5. Buyer would have to pay stamp duty, legal fees, mortgage valuation, and all other costs out of own resources as these cannot be included in the mortgage or property bank loan.

6. Property would be registered at the land registry with a value of £200,000 if sale went ahead.

7. Sale does not go ahead because the maximum amount the Buyer is willing to pay is £197,000.

Scenario two based on The Price Strategy

1. Asking price: £210,000 with no stamp duty to pay (i.e. the Seller pays the stamp duty).

2. Discounted amount (price agreed after negotiation): £200,000, but Buyer pays stamp duty.

3. Cash Incentive agreed (payment from Seller to Buyer): £10,000 (difference between £210,000 and £200,000, so Seller ends up getting £200,000 for house).

4. Mortgage amount is £199,500 (95% of £210,000).

5. Mortgage Deposit (payment from Buyer to Buyer's Lender): £10,500 (5% of £210,000).

6. Buyer can pay for stamp duty, legal fees, mortgage valuation, and all other costs from the Cash Incentive, and still have thousands of pounds left over.

7. Property is registered at the land registry with a value of £210,000, giving the Buyer more equity.

We will now look at scenario two in more detail and explain the strategy further. At the beginning of this chapter a three-step procedure is described for a person buying property. Similarly, what follows is a three-step procedure that a **Seller** should follow:

STEP 1: Negotiate a price.

STEP 2: Make an offer.

STEP 3: Confirm it in writing.

STEP 1: Negotiate a price.

- The Seller will naturally negotiate the best price he can get should a Buyer not agree to the asking price. There may come a point when the Seller has to say he will reduce the price provided the Buyer pays the stamp duty. If a price is agreed, that is the end of the matter and you don't go on to steps 2 and 3. If a price cannot be agreed the Seller can use *The Price Strategy* to bridge the price gap and clinch a deal that will be good for both the Seller and the Buyer.

- To summarize STEP 1, the Seller will go on to STEP 2 only if the negotiations are not getting anywhere or if the Seller wants to get things moving quickly and reach an agreement.

STEP 2: Make an offer.

You go on to this step only if you have not been able to agree a price in the conventional manner. At this point the dialogue and negotiations would go something like this:

- *'I have said that I cannot go below £200,000 and you have said that you cannot offer more than £197,000 and on top of that pay the cost of stamp duty. As we haven't been able to agree a price I would like to make you a special offer that will benefit both of us. It would enable you to buy this house and end up with spare cash to pay for legal fees, stamp duty, and anything else you like. Are you interested?'*

- *'I want to ask you to agree to a selling price of £210,000. Don't worry, you won't actually be paying this price for the house, but the transaction would go through as £210,000.'*

- *'So the price of £210,000 is the price that would go on all the paperwork including your mortgage application. This will be the Open Market Value and the agreed SELLING PRICE between us. As a result, you will get a mortgage based on £210,000 rather than on £197,000. This is a perfectly legal and proper way to proceed. And provided the VALUATION of the house carried out by your Lender is not less than £210,000 you will get your mortgage based on this figure.'*

- *'This means you will get £10,000 more than you need to buy the house. So you get a loan for 210,000, you pay me £200,000, and you have £10,000 left over. This £10,000 is called a Cash Incentive. In practice what would happen is that your solicitor pays my solicitor £210,000 because this is the selling price. Then my solicitor gives my Cash Incentive to you via your solicitor. You will be able to use this additional money for anything you like.'*

At this point it is essential to make sure the Buyer understands how the Cash Incentive works. Explain that the Cash Incentive is a payment from the Buyer to himself. But the Cash Incentive money goes to the Buyer *via the Seller*. (See the money-flow diagram given in an earlier part of this chapter.)

To finish this point, the Seller should explain that the cash incentive is surplus money left over from the mortgage loan (the difference between the amount borrowed and the amount actually paid for the property). Here is an example of how the negotiations for the Seller might proceed:

- *'Of course, you will need to tell your solicitor that although you have agreed a PRICE of £210,000, you are only expecting to pay £200,000 because you are getting a £10,000 Cash Incentive from me, the Seller. I'll give you a letter that you can send to your solicitor which explains this.'*

- *'As I said, this is completely legal and above board, and is common practice in the building industry. The £10,000 price difference is called a 'Cash Incentive' and any experienced conveyancer will be familiar with this way of doing business. As mentioned, this £10,000 is a Cash Incentive from me to you but the money does not originate from me – it comes from your own mortgage (from the money you are borrowing to buy this house).'*

- *'Have a look at these advertisements. What I am proposing is no different to the way that large building companies operate. You and I are doing the same thing but on a smaller scale. In these advertisements, the building companies are selling direct to buyers just like I am selling direct to you.'*

(Show advertisements depicting Cash Incentive offers from builders like Barratt. Answer any remaining questions.)

- *'Let's summarize what you get out of the deal:*

  1. *You get to buy this house (or 'my house') instead of losing it to another Buyer.*

  2. *You get £10,000 cash-in-hand for spending on anything you like. If you wanted to, this money could finance your mortgage deposit, or be put into a high interest savings account to offset mortgage interest payments. It could certainly be used to pay for legal costs and stamp duty, and enable you to buy this house for little or no money down.*

3. *You get to buy a property at below market value (a good bargain). This is so because you're buying a property valued at £210,000 but only paying £200,000.*

4. *You get a property with equity, i.e. the potential profit that can be made when re-selling the property. The equity is the difference between the market value and the amount owing on the property. For example, if you are getting a 95% mortgage on £210,000, you will owe 95% of £210,000 which is £199,500. And if the market value is, say, £210,000, the equity is £10,500.'*

- *'So can I take it that you agree in principle with this strategy? If so, I will give you some information for sending to your solicitor.'*

(Wait for Buyer to respond. You need to get a verbal agreement before proceeding.)

Summary of the Seller benefits:

1. Seller has found a Buyer and can sell the house.

2. Seller gets to sell the house at the desired price.

3. Seller's house is not devalued in the local market place (this can benefit the Seller if he owns other local properties, or has nearby relatives who own properties).

Summary of the Buyer benefits:

1. Buyer gets a property at below market value (a good bargain).

2. Buyer gets to buy the property at a bargain price because, as a result of getting the Cash Incentive, he paid much less than the registered price.

3. Buyer gets a property with equity, i.e. the potential profit that can be made when re-selling the property.

4. Buyer gets cash (in this example £10,000) that can be used to pay for stamp duty, legal fees, conveyancing costs, or just be put into a savings account!). In some cases the savings can be

enough for the Buyer to acquire a property with 'no money down'.

TIP

Benefits Sheet

Prepare a sheet of paper that just shows the four Buyer benefits. Use a large size font and use the word 'you' instead of 'Buyer'. Give the *Benefits Sheet* to the Buyer as you mention these benefits.

Remember that the key to *The Price Strategy* is the difference between the Selling Price you have agreed (and which the buyer's mortgage is applied to) and the actual amount paid to the Seller. This difference is the cash incentive (not to be confused with a *'gifted deposit'* described earlier) and is common practice in the building industry. Ideally the cash incentive should not be more than 5% to 10% of the PRICE. If it is not over 5% (as in this example) it is more likely to be accepted by most Lenders. Note that cash incentives of 15% or more are not uncommon in the building industry.

Note: The Buyer should always declare the *Cash Incentive* on his mortgage application form (there is nothing to hide). Most Lenders will usually not mind that the Buyer is getting a cash incentive provided the selling price is in line with the valuation report. Remember three things: (i) The *Cash Incentive* is not an additional loan from the Lender, (ii) the Lender is not involved with the Cash Incentive in any direct or legal sense, and (iii) Lenders themselves give Cash Incentives to Buyers (just look at any mortgage magazine).

As a Seller, you would be using the same *Price Strategies* employed by many well known house building companies. There is absolutely nothing underhand about this strategy – it is perfectly legal and proper. Private individuals have the same right to use this strategy as much as house-building companies do. So when you meet a Buyer who tries to negotiate a lower price, do your best to agree a price. But if a price cannot be agreed and there is a price gap to bridge, use *The Price Strategy* to your mutual advantage.

However, it is important that the Buyer is aware that some Lenders do not accept private vendor cash incentives. It may be necessary for him to speak to a suitably qualified mortgage broker.

Make sure that when you put the property up for sale you brief your solicitor about your intention to offer a 'Cash Incentive' should it be necessary in your negotiations. Do this *before* putting the property on the market. If your solicitor is not familiar with the concept of a 'Cash Incentive' in a property transaction you should perhaps find another solicitor. Then, if a Buyer needs reassurance about the strategy, you can tell the Buyer to ask his solicitor to contact your solicitor to get confirmation that a Cash Incentive is a perfectly acceptable way of proceeding.

STEP 3: Confirm it in writing.

Let's recap. In step 1 you negotiated the best price possible in the conventional manner but you were unable to agree a selling price with the Buyer. In step 2 you made an offer based on *The Price Strategy* and you got a positive response indicating co-operation with the strategy. Now, in step 3 you will be giving the Buyer two letters.

The first letter is a written confirmation from you to the Buyer to clarify the offer you have just made. This first letter would be issued in duplicate so that the Buyer can sign and return one copy to indicate an agreement in principle to proceed. Try to get the letter signed there and then (otherwise it can be posted to you).

The second letter is a draft letter for the Buyer to send to his solicitor to get things moving. Both these letters are shown below, with suggested wording that can be adapted as necessary.

Note: These two letters would also be copied to any estate agent that may be involved in the transaction.

Price confirmation letter from Seller to Buyer

(date)

From: (Seller's name and address)

To: (Buyer's name and address)

Re: Sale of my property *(enter property address)*

Following our meeting, I confirm that we have agreed in principle the following price details for the sale of my house:

SELLING PRICE: **(Price agreed for selling property)**	*£ (enter agreed price)* *[Note: In the case of the above example, this would be £210,000]*
***Less Cash Incentive to buyer:** **(For redecoration, repairs, and miscellaneous costs)**	*£ (enter agreed amount)* *[Note: In the case of the above example, this would be £10,000]*
Total cash on completion:	*£ (enter difference of above two figures)* *[Note: In the case of the above example, this would be £200,000]*

*The Cash Incentive referred to above is a sum of money that will be paid from the Seller's solicitor to the Buyer's solicitor on completion of the property transaction.

The address of my solicitor is as follows: (enter Seller's solicitor details).

I confirm that the Buyer will declare the Cash Incentive on his mortgage application form. (Delete this paragraph if Buyer is not using a loan to buy the property.)

It is understood that the sale of my house is subject to contract, and a satisfactory valuation if it is being bought with a mortgage. The next step is to tell your solicitor to buy this property from me as detailed above.

[THE FOLLOWING PARAGRAPH APPLIES ONLY IF AN ESTATE AGENT IS INVOLVED]:

I confirm I will ask my estate agent to issue a 'memorandum of sale' and withdraw the property from the market. I will make clear to the estate agent that the SELLING PRICE is the higher amount (before deduction of the Cash Incentive). No discount applies to this transaction and the word 'discount' should not appear on any documentation as this would be incorrect. I will ask the estate agent to send a copy of the memorandum of sale to you so that you can ask your Lender to carry out the mortgage valuation of my property. Please sign the declaration below and give me a copy of this letter to indicate that you agree in principle to buy my property as explained above. I will then be able to withdraw the property from the market.

[THE FOLLOWING PARAGRAPH APPLIES ONLY IF AN ESTATE AGENT IS **NOT** INVOLVED]:

As no estate agent is involved in this transaction, this letter takes the place of the memorandum of sale. Please sign the declaration below and give me a copy of this letter to indicate that you agree in principle to buy my property as explained above. I will then be able to withdraw the property from the market.

If anything is not clear please contact me at any time.

Yours sincerely,

(name of Seller)

DECLARATION BY BUYER: *I agree in principle to BUY your property on the terms described above, subject to valuation and subject to contract.*

Signed: ....Date:..................

Print Name: ....

Letter from Buyer to Buyer's solicitor

Dear (Solicitor)

Property: *(Address)*

I have asked you to act for me in the purchase of a property. I am now writing to explain that I wish to buy the above named property and the details are as follows:

1. *Name of Seller: (enter name).*

2. *Seller's solicitor: (enter name, address, and telephone number).*

3. *Price for buying property: (enter SELLING PRICE, not discounted amount).*

4. *Cash Incentive: I have also agreed to receive a Cash Incentive of £ (enter amount). This sum of money is to be paid to me upon completion, from the mortgage amount that I will be borrowing.*

I confirm that I will declare the Cash Incentive on my mortgage application form. (Delete this paragraph if Buyer is not using a loan to buy the property.)

Please find enclosed a copy of a price confirmation letter I have received from the Seller.

Yours sincerely

(name of Buyer)

The second letter, from the Buyer to his solicitor, is important as it will focus the Buyer's mind into taking the correct action and being committed to following the strategy.

If the Buyer will not sign the declaration in the letter there and then, you should allow the Buyer to take the letter away, and consult their solicitor should they wish to. In this event, you should make it clear that you cannot take the property off the market until the letter is signed or until you get a clear indication of an intention to buy.

Important Note: *When mentioning this strategy to a solicitor, only talk in terms of giving a Cash Incentive to the Buyer. Do not talk in terms of giving a cashback that is deducted from the Buyer's mortgage money, as this is not the case, and solicitors may regard this as somewhat dubious. Also, point out that the Buyer will be declaring the cash incentive on his mortgage application form, and that this is no different to the Cash Incentives given by house-building companies, a practice that is common all over the UK.*

The Price Strategy then, is using the Buyer's mortgage company to in effect give the Buyer cash in hand. In doing this, the Buyer is able to proceed at a higher price than otherwise. From the Buyer's point of view, it is much better, for example, to end up with a mortgage of £199,500 and have £10,000 cash in hand, than to end up with a mortgage of £190,000 and no cash in hand.

The Buyer may end up paying a little more in monthly interest on a mortgage of £199,500 compared to £190,000, but the difference is relatively small compared with the advantage of having cash in hand. If the mortgage interest is 5% the monthly payment would be about £831 compared with £792 (a difference of about £39). The Buyer doesn't have to spend all of the Cash Incentive – he could put some of the money into a high-interest savings account to offset the small increase in monthly interest.

You may point out to the Buyer that he may use the cash incentive money for any purpose he wishes. The main advantage, of course, is the fact that the Buyer gets to receive cash at a time when he may most need it to finance the property transaction.

If a Buyer is buying his home with limited savings and limited income, a Cash Incentive can sometimes make or break a property deal. For the Buyer, *The Price Strategy* will improve cash flow, particularly if a buy-to-let property is involved. In this scenario, the Buyer's small increase in monthly interest will not matter as much since he gets tax relief on mortgage interest.

The big question for a Seller

How does the Seller persuade the Buyer to get a bigger mortgage as a means of getting a Cash Incentive (and pay more for the property)? After all, that is what *The Price Strategy* is all about. This is how:

Step one: Set a realistic open market value.

- Before putting the property up for sale establish a realistic open market value for your property. Then base your selling price on this. Do this by talking to estate agents or by checking the prices of similar properties in the area. Then set your asking price to include the cost of stamp duty. Either decide that you will absorb this cost, or put the price up to compensate for this cost (or do 'half and half').

- Including stamp duty in the price of a house is a good way of attracting interest and it will make your offer stand out from the other properties in the area. If you are using an estate agent they can make your property stand out from the others by featuring the free stamp duty. Clearly, if you put the price up to include the stamp duty, the Buyer will, in effect, end up paying this cost. But, by doing this, the Buyer will be able to pay the stamp duty using mortgage money instead of his own money.

TIP

Offering to sell a property free of stamp duty is a good marketing strategy. But to do this you must decide whether to put the price up to compensate for the cost of stamp duty, or whether to absorb the cost yourself as a way of generating greater buyer interest (or doing a bit of both). Although it can be quite effective to offer property free of stamp duty, there is no clear-cut answer to this issue as it depends on local property market conditions and your personal circumstances. If you are selling through an estate agent, get their advice on this matter.

- Establish your minimum price: have a clear figure in mind and make this your rock bottom price below which you will not sell. This figure should not include the cost of stamp duty. Your objective is to get your asking price or a price between your asking price and your minimum price. If a buyer will not meet your minimum price, you would then use *The Price Strategy*.

Step two: Be flexible on price.

Make it clear to all and sundry (potential buyers, advertisements, estate agents, leaflets, etc) that you will accept offers, or that you can be flexible on the price. The abbreviation O.N.O. (Or Near Offer) can be used when stating the price. You want a Buyer to be willing to negotiate with you because you can then use *The Price Strategy* if a deal cannot be agreed.

Step three: Be prepared.

Make sure you are prepared with all the paperwork that you need. Prepare a folder containing all the documents relating to *The Price Strategy*. These are:

1. The Buyer benefits sheet.

2. Money-flow diagram (as given in this chapter).

3. Samples of house-building company advertisements showing Cash Incentive offers (check property newspapers, magazines, etc).

4. Price confirmation letter from Seller to Buyer.

5. Letter from Buyer to Buyer's solicitor.

Step four: Use the Strategy.

Apply *The Price Strategy* exactly as explained in this chapter. Point out the benefits to the Buyer. These are genuine benefits – it's a 'win, win' solution for both the Buyer and the Seller. Remember: Use the strategy as a last resort. *Do not use the strategy if a price can be agreed in the conventional manner.* But note the following: If a buyer says he is willing to agree the price but does not have enough ready cash to pay for the mortgage deposit, the *stamp duty,* the legal fees, etc. then consider proposing *The Price Strategy* to make it possible for the Buyer to do business with you.

Combining Two Amounts

You can combine the discount amount and the stamp duty amount to give the Buyer a bigger Cash Incentive than otherwise (with no loss to the Seller).

To clarify this further, here is an example:

Example

1. The asking price is £210,000.

2. **Discount amount £5,000.** After negotiation you agree a price reduction of £5,000, bringing the price down to £205,000.

3. **Stamp duty amount £2,000.** The stamp duty on £210,000 at 1% is £2,100, so the Seller can increase the selling price by, say, £2,000 (from £210,000 to £212,000).

4. The Seller can then offer a Cash Incentive of £7,000 (the total of the discount amount of £5,000 and the stamp duty amount of £2,000).

5. The Seller gets paid the agreed £205,000 and the Buyer gets a mortgage based on £212,000 with a Cash Incentive of £7,000.

Most property transactions are likely to involve combining two amounts in this way, to give as big a Cash Incentive as possible. These two amounts are: (i) the difference between the asking price and the reduced price negotiated, and (ii) the difference between the asking price and a higher price based on adding the stamp duty.

When these two elements (the discount amount and the stamp duty amount) are combined, this makes for a very powerful and effective strategy. Remember that a big Cash Incentive for the buyer means that the Seller can offer or negotiate better terms.

Summary of *The Price Strategy* for a Buyer:

1. Brief your solicitor about the use of a 'Cash Incentive' for buying your next property. Say that you will be asking the Seller to give you a small Cash Incentive upon completion. Should you need to explain further, go through the example at the beginning of this chapter. You should not need to explain the whole strategy. If the solicitor is not familiar with the concept of a Cash Incentive find another. The purpose here is to 'prime' your solicitor to be receptive and to fully co-operate with the Seller's solicitor when the time comes. Any experienced conveyancer will be familiar with the concept of a Cash Incentive.

2. Find a mortgage broker who can find you the best possible mortgage which will allow a Cash Incentive from the Seller.

3. Find a property and negotiate the best price reduction possible. Use *The Price Strategy*, whether or not a price reduction can be obtained. If a price reduction is granted, ask the Seller for a Cash Incentive equivalent to the price reduction. If no price reduction is granted, ask the Seller for a Cash Incentive equivalent to the amount of stamp duty (you do this by asking the Seller to increase the SELLING PRICE by an amount equivalent to the stamp duty).

4. Offer the Seller an additional £300 (or some other amount) to encourage his co-operation. Do this by offering to buy a low-value item (or items) in the property for £300, and say this will be a separate cash transaction between you and the Seller.

5. Show the Seller one or more advertisements used by building companies such as Barratt, offering Cash Incentives in the form of money, stamp duty payments, and so on. Explain that what you are proposing is no different to the way that large building companies operate, but on a smaller scale. Explain that a Cash Incentive is a perfectly legal and common way of doing business.

6. Make full use of a combined strategy to get as big a Cash Incentive as possible. Do this by combining the discount amount with the stamp duty amount. That way you will always get a Cash Incentive, even when little or no price reduction can be obtained.

7. Tell Seller the next step is to inform their solicitor (and estate agent if applicable). Do this by using the two sample letters given above.

8. Follow through with all parties (Seller, Estate Agent, Solicitor, Lender) to get things moving.

Summary of *The Price Strategy* for a Seller:

1. Brief your solicitor about the use of a *'Cash Incentive'* for selling your property.

2. Use *The Price Strategy* as a last resort (i.e. when the price required cannot be obtained).

3. Show the Buyer several cash incentive advertisements used by well-known building companies. Explain that a Cash Incentive in the building industry is a perfectly legal and ethical way of doing business. Make sure the Buyer speaks to a good mortgage broker who can advise him of the options.

4. Explain the money flow diagram (see diagram in this chapter) to ensure full understanding.

5. Make full use of a combined strategy to offer as big a *Cash Incentive* as possible. Do this by combining the discount amount with the stamp duty amount. That way you will always be able to offer a Cash Incentive, even when little or no price reduction can be offered.

6. Agree the strategy with the Buyer. If necessary say: *'Will you agree to buy my house based on a selling price of £XYZ and a Cash Incentive to you of £ABC?'* When the buyer agrees or shows serious interest, give him the two letter documents.

The Valuation Strategy

The Valuation Strategy is one of the best ways of saving stamp duty costs and other property purchase costs. It's a 'win, win' situation for all concerned, and as you will see, a strategy that should be applied to virtually all property purchases.

This strategy is based on the principle of getting a full market valuation for the property (the higher the valuation the better). A good (i.e. high) valuation will result in a more favourable loan, increased equity, higher profits, and better cash flow. Let's briefly look at the financial elements that go into this strategy.

PRICE (or SELLING PRICE). Normally, when a PRICE is agreed between Buyer and Seller, this is the figure that goes on your mortgage application form. And provided that the valuation carried out by the LENDER is not *less* than the PRICE, you will get a mortgage based on this figure.

AMOUNT PAID. This is the reduced price that has been negotiated and agreed upon, and is the actual amount of money that the Seller will end up getting for the property. Note that the LOAN is based on the PRICE (not the AMOUNT PAID), provided the VALUATION is not lower than the PRICE.

VALUATION. This is the open market value deemed to apply to the property by the LENDER. So here we are not talking about a valuation carried out by an estate agent or anybody else (unless employed by the LENDER to do the valuation). Rather, it is based on the resell value and not the cost of rebuilding. Should the property be repossessed, the LENDER wants evidence that money will be recouped by reselling the property.

LENDER. The mortgage company or bank that is lending money to the buyer as a secured loan, i.e. the loan is secured on the property.

COMPARABLE. This stands for 'comparable price'. It refers to another property near the one you want to buy (same postal district or within one to two miles), that is similar in type and price. So if you have three comparables, it means you have information on three other properties that can be compared to the property you are buying or selling in terms of price and type of property. Comparables do not have to be physically identical to the property being sold, just roughly similar, so that like is compared with like.

Coming back to the VALUATION, the sequence of events leading up to the valuation is as follows:

1. Find a property you want to buy.

2. Agree a price.

3. Seller and Buyer both instruct solicitors.

4. Buyer applies for a mortgage.

5. Lender carries out a valuation and if satisfactory (i.e. not lower than the PRICE) a mortgage is granted.

The *Valuation Strategy* involves getting as high a valuation as possible in order to fully reflect the open market value of the property. This is perfectly legal and proper, as no misrepresentation of the value is involved.

The following example explains the strategy further:

Example

- Seller's asking price: £230,000

- Rock bottom amount that Seller is willing to accept after negotiation: £228,000

- For this example we assume a valuation of £238,000

- Buyer can get a 95% Loan to Value mortgage. Deposit is therefore 5%

In this example we will compare two scenarios:

Scenario one, based on the traditional approach

1. Original asking price: £230,000

2. Amount paid (price agreed after negotiation): £228,000.

3. Agreed selling price: £228,000.

4. Mortgage amount is £216,600 (95% of £228,000).

5. Mortgage Deposit (payment from Buyer to Buyer's Lender): £11,400 (5% of £228,000).

6. Buyer has to pay stamp duty, legal fees, mortgage valuation, and all other costs out of own resources as these cannot be included in the mortgage loan.

7. Property is registered at the land registry with a value of £228,000.

 ### Scenario two based on The Valuation Strategy

1. Original asking price: £230,000

2. Amount paid (price agreed after negotiation): £228,000.

3. Agreed selling price: £238,000 (£10,000 more than the amount to be paid after negotiating a price reduction).

4. Cash Incentive agreed (payment from Seller to Buyer): £10,000 (difference between £238,000 and £228,000, thereby Seller gets £228,000 for house).

5. Mortgage amount is £226,100 (95% of £238,000).

6. Mortgage Deposit (payment from Buyer to Buyer's Lender): £11,900 (5% of £238,000).

7. Buyer can pay stamp duty, legal fees, mortgage valuation, and all other costs from the £10,000 Cash Incentive, and still have money left over.

8. Property is registered at the land registry with a value of £238,000.

Same as Valuation

We will now look at scenario two in more detail and explain the strategy further. What follows is a step-by-step procedure, including suggested dialogue. There are three steps to follow.

STEP 1: Negotiate a price.

STEP 2: Make an offer.

STEP 3: Confirm it in writing.

STEP 1: Negotiate a price.

The Buyer and Seller will negotiate a price in the usual manner. It is assumed in this example that a price reduction of £2,000 has been agreed, making the amount to pay £228,000. Note, however, that *The Valuation Strategy* can be used even where no price reduction is forthcoming, or where there is a price gap to bridge.

STEP 2: Make an offer.

The Seller may think that negotiations are over, but for the Buyer this is where the negotiations start and *The Valuation Strategy* now springs into action.

Having clearly agreed a price reduction to £228,000, you now ask the Seller to agree a SELLING PRICE of £238,000. This apparent *volte-face* may come as a surprise to the Seller, but the Buyer goes on to explain that the price to be paid will still only be £228,000. The dialogue would go along the lines that follow:

Dialogue:

- *'Now that we've agreed a price of £228,000 this is the amount I will be paying you. I like your house very much and it shouldn't be devalued. I want to enter the full market value at the Land Registry. Therefore I want to ask you to agree a selling price of £238,000. I also want to ask you to give me a Cash Incentive of £10,000. This means you get the agreed £228,000, but the house value will go through on the Land Registry as £238,000.'*

86

Note: You will have arrived at a figure of £238,000 having researched the values of similar properties in the area (more on this later).

- *'The house price of £238,000 is the price that would go on all the paperwork including my mortgage application. This will help me cover legal fees, stamp duty, and other costs such as certain renovation work before I move in.'*

- *'This method of buying your house won't affect you in any way. On completion, my solicitor will give your solicitor the agreed selling price of £238,000. Your solicitor will then give my solicitor the £10,000 Cash Incentive. Of course, you will need to tell your solicitor about this so I will give you a letter that explains everything.'*

- *'All that we have discussed is completely legal and above board, and is common practice throughout the building industry. The £10,000 price difference is called a 'Cash Incentive', and any experienced conveyancer will be familiar with this way of doing business. This £10,000 is a Cash Incentive from you to me, but the money does not come from you – it comes from the money I am borrowing to buy your house.'*

- *'The Cash Incentive is, in effect, a payment from my Lender to me, but it goes through you. Have a look at this diagram.'* (see Fig. 7)

To finish this point, explain that the Cash Incentive amounts to surplus money left over from the mortgage loan (the difference between the amount borrowed and the amount actually paid for the property). You now continue the dialogue to finish the negotiations.

- *'Have a look at these advertisements. What I am proposing is no different to the way that large building companies operate. You and I are doing the same thing but on a smaller scale. In these advertisements, the building companies are selling direct to buyers, just as you are selling direct to me.'*

(Show advertisements depicting Cash Incentive offers from builders like Barratt. Answer any remaining questions).

Fig. 7 - Money-flow Diagram

Step 1

LENDER
(Money loaned to Buyer, based on selling price)

Step 2

BUYER'S SOLICITOR
(Money given to Buyer's solicitor for buying property)

Step 3

SELLER'S SOLICITOR
(Money paid to Seller's solicitor on completion, without deducting
the Cash Incentive)

Step 4

BUYER'S SOLICITOR
(Seller's solicitor 'pays' Cash Incentive money to Buyer's solicitor
for giving to Buyer)

Step 5

BUYER
Buyer receives Cash Incentive money as part of the final
reconciliation of the completion statement prepared
by the Buyer's solicitor

- *'If you can help me out by doing this I will be very pleased to buy your (fridge/curtains/sofa/flower pots/whatever) for £300. I will pay you cash for these items as a separate transaction. So you will end up getting the £228,000 payment for the house, and in addition you get a separate cash payment direct from me for £300.'*

Make sure that you have established beforehand in your own mind which item (or items) you will be buying for £300. It needs to be an item of little value, or an item that would have been included in the price of the house anyway. That way, the £300 will be genuinely appreciated.

- *'If you will agree to this method of selling your property this is how you will benefit:*

  1. *You get to sell your property at the agreed price.*

  2. *You can stop looking for a buyer.*

  3. *Your property will not be devalued in the local market place as it will be registered at the higher value of £238,000. This can benefit you or your relatives who may own other properties in the area.*

  4. *You get an additional £300 as a separate cash payment direct from me.'*

(Give the Seller a separate sheet showing these four benefits).

- *'So can I take it that you agree in principle with this strategy? If so, I will give you a letter confirming my agreement to buy your house. I will also give you a letter that you can send to your solicitor which explains the strategy we have been talking about.'*

Stop to make sure the Seller has heard you correctly, and make certain there are no misunderstandings. At this point you must wait to get an answer to know whether or not the Seller is going to co-operate. Do not proceed to STEP 3 if it is clear that the Seller will not co-operate.

The benefits to the Seller are:

1. Seller has found a Buyer and can sell the house.

2. Seller gets a bonus, e.g. £300.

3. Seller's house is not devalued in the local market place.

The benefits to the Buyer are:

1. Buyer gets a property at below market value (a good bargain).

2. Buyer gets a property with equity, i.e. the potential profit that can be made when re-selling the property.

3. Buyer gets cash (in this example £10,000 less £300) that can be used to pay for stamp duty, legal fees, conveyancing costs, or just be put into a savings account!).

TIP

Prepare a sheet of paper that just shows the four Buyer benefits. Use a large size font and use the word 'you' instead of 'Buyer'. Give this sheet to the Buyer when you mention these benefits.

The key to *The Valuation Strategy* is the price difference between the 'official' price on which the mortgage is based, and the actual amount paid to the Seller. This difference is the *cash incentive*. In the building industry it is common for house builders to offer cash incentives, and the amount of the cash incentive will have been factored into the selling price. Hence, there is no legal difference between a cash incentive offered by a house builder and a cash incentive offered by a private individual as described in this strategy.

Ideally the cash incentive should not be more than 5% to 10% of the PRICE. If it is not over 5% (as in this example) it is more likely to be accepted by most Lenders. Note that cash incentives of 15% or more are not uncommon in the building industry.

However, some Lenders will not accept cash incentives from private Sellers to it is essential that you speak with a mortgage broker before proceeding with this strategy.

Note: The Buyer should always declare the *cash incentive* on his mortgage application form (there is nothing to hide). Most Lenders will usually not mind that the Buyer is getting a cash incentive provided the selling price is in line with the valuation report. Remember three things: (i) The *Cash Incentive* is not an additional loan from the Lender, (ii) the Lender is not involved with the cash incentive in any direct or legal sense, and (iii) Lenders themselves give cash incentives to Buyers (just look at any mortgage magazine).

To reassure the Seller about this way of doing business, explain that virtually all house building companies operate this way. Show the Seller some typical advertisements (as illustrated earlier).

The Valuation Strategy uses the same strategy employed by many other property builders. In the example at the beginning of this chapter, the Seller is giving you, the Buyer, a £10,000 Cash Incentive in return for buying their property.

Thus when you apply *The Valuation Strategy* you are, in effect, enabling the Seller to use the same selling methods used by large national builders. There is absolutely nothing underhand about this strategy – it is perfectly legal and proper. Private individuals have the same right to use this strategy as much as house-building companies do. So when you go to meet a Seller to negotiate a price, go equipped with advertisements from builders such as Barratt.

Note that if using a Cash Incentive to finance a mortgage deposit, a Buyer may have to obtain a bridging loan for two or three days (the time interval between paying the deposit to the solicitor to complete the deal and receiving the Cash Incentive to repay the bridging loan).

Make sure that you brief your solicitor about your plan to ask a Buyer for a *Cash Incentive* if you cannot get the price you want. Do this *before* you start to look for a property to buy. If your solicitor is not familiar with the concept of a *Cash Incentive* in a property transaction you should perhaps find another solicitor. Then, if a Seller needs reassurance about the strategy, you can tell the Seller to ask his solicitor to contact your solicitor to get confirmation that the *Cash Incentive* is a perfectly acceptable way of proceeding.

STEP 3: Confirm it in writing.

Let's recap. In step 1 you negotiated the best possible price in the conventional manner. In step 2 you made an offer based on *The Valuation Strategy* and you got a positive response indicating cooperation with the strategy. Now, in step 3 you will be giving the Seller two letters.

The first letter is a written confirmation from you to the Seller to clarify the offer you have just made. This first letter would be issued in duplicate so that the Seller can sign and return one copy to indicate an agreement in principle to proceed.

The second letter is a draft letter for the Seller to send to his solicitor to get things moving. Both these letters are shown below, with suggested wording that can be adapted as necessary.

Written confirmation of offer from Buyer to Seller

(date)

From: (Buyer's name and address)

To: (Seller's name and address)

Re: Sale of your property *(enter property address)*

Following my viewing of your property, I would like to make a formal offer made up as follows:

Full Offer Price:	*£ (enter agreed price)* *[Note: In the case of our example, this would be £238,000]*
*Less Cash Incentive: **(For redecoration, repairs, and miscellaneous costs)**	*£ (enter agreed amount)* *[Note: In the case of our example, this would be £10,000]*
Total cash on completion:	*£ (enter difference of above two figures)* *[Note: In the case of the our example, this would be £228,000]*

*The Cash Incentive referred to above is a sum of money that will be paid from the Seller's solicitor to the Buyer's solicitor on completion of the property transaction.

The address of my solicitor is as follows: (enter Buyer's solicitor details).

I confirm that I will declare the Cash Incentive on my mortgage application form. (Delete this paragraph if Buyer is not using a loan to buy the property.)

This offer is subject to satisfactory valuation and contract. The next step is to tell your solicitor to sell your property to me as explained above.

If an estate agent is involved, you need to ask the estate agent to issue a 'memorandum of sale' and withdraw the property from the market. ***Please ensure that your estate agent clearly understands that the SELLING PRICE is the higher amount (before deduction of the Cash Incentive).*** *No discount applies to this transaction and the word 'discount' should not appear on any documentation as this would be incorrect. When I receive a copy of the memorandum of sale I will ask my Lender to carry out the mortgage valuation on the property.*

Please sign the declaration below and give me a copy of this letter to indicate that you agree in principle to sell me your house on the terms given above.

If anything is not clear please contact me at any time.

Yours sincerely,

(enter Buyer's name)

DECLARATION BY SELLER: *I agree to sell you my property on the terms described above, subject to valuation and subject to contract.*

Signed:.....................................Date:...........

Print Name: ....

Letter from Seller to Seller's solicitor

Dear (Solicitor)

Property: *(Address)*

I have asked you to act for me in the selling of my above property. I am writing to explain that I have found a buyer and the details are as follows:

1. *Name of buyer: (enter name).*

2. *Buyer's solicitor: (enter name, address, and telephone number).*

3. *Price for selling property: (enter SELLING PRICE, not discounted amount).*

4. *Cash Incentive: I have also agreed to give the buyer a Cash Incentive of £ (enter amount). This sum of money is to be paid to the buyer upon completion, from the proceeds of sale. This means that the total cash on completion will be £xyz (the agreed price of £..... less the Cash Incentive of £.....).*

Please find enclosed a copy of the offer I have received from the buyer.

Yours sincerely

(name of Seller)

The second letter, from the Seller to his solicitor, is important as it will focus the Seller's mind into taking the correct action and being committed to following the strategy.

If the Seller will not sign the declaration in the letter there and then, you should allow the Seller to consult a solicitor. In this event, you the Buyer should make it clear that you cannot commit to buying the property, or stop looking at other properties, until the letter is signed or until you get a clear indication of an intention to sell the property to you.

Important Note: *When mentioning this strategy to a solicitor, only talk in terms of getting a Cash Incentive from the Seller. Do not talk in terms of getting a cashback from the Lender as this is not the case, and solicitors may regard this as somewhat dubious. Also, point out that you will be declaring the cash incentive on the mortgage application form, and that this is no different to getting a Cash Incentive from a house-building company, a practice that is common all over the UK.*

The Valuation Strategy then, is using the *Lender's money* rather than your own money (assuming you have any!) to pay for stamp duty and other costs. In the above example it is much better to end up with a mortgage of £226,100, and have £10,000 cash-in-hand, than to end up with a mortgage of £216,600, and no cash-in-hand.

You may end up paying a little more in monthly interest on a mortgage of £226,100 compared witho £216,600, but the difference is relatively small compared with the advantage of having cash in hand.

When buying a home with limited savings and limited income, a Cash Incentive from the Seller can sometimes make or break a property deal. Remember: this is a *Cash Incentive,* not a *Mortgage Cashback.* If the mortgage company itself is providing a cashback you get two cashbacks! One from the Seller, and one from the Lender.

If you are running a buy-to-let business, *The Valuation Strategy* will improve your cash flow and give you more equity. And the small increase in monthly interest will not matter as much since the interest should be allowed as a tax deduction.

96

The Big Question

We now come to the question of how best to get a full market valuation? In the above example, a valuation of £238,000 is needed for this strategy to work. If the valuation carried out by the Lender is different to the PRICE what will happen?

If the VALUATION is less than the PRICE, the Lender will either say NO to the LOAN, or offer a reduced LOAN based on the lower VALUATION.

If the VALUATION is the same as, or higher than the PRICE, the Lender will grant the LOAN applied for. Note that the Valuer will usually try to make the valuation match the PRICE, knowing that this is most advantageous to both the Lender and the Buyer.

When you apply for a mortgage you will be stating the PRICE on the application form, e.g. £238,000. The Lender then instructs a local estate agent or Valuation company to carry out a valuation. Note that although you, the Buyer, are paying for the valuation, the Valuer is working for the Lender and reports back to the Lender.

So how do you make sure that you get the VALUATION that you need? This is how:

Step one: check out local property prices

- Before you make an offer on the property, and before you negotiate a reduction, find out the approximate values of similar properties in the area. Do this by enquiring at local estate agents, by checking local property newspapers, and by walking or driving around the area looking for other properties for sale or sold. Finding COMPARABLES is at the heart of the strategy.

TIP

Whenever you visit a potential property always be on the look-out for other properties being offered for sale or already sold in the area (make a note of the addresses). Later, these addresses can prove very useful if you need comparables.

- If this initial research reveals several more highly priced properties that could be COMPARABLES, you know you may be able to apply *The Valuation Strategy*. If you find that there are no similar properties at higher prices and if you feel that the target property is not undervalued, you should consider not applying *The Valuation Strategy*. If you find that comparable prices are *lower* rather than higher, use this information to negotiate a lower price and apply *The Price Strategy* instead. Either way, your time will not be wasted.

Step two: Use the internet to get comparables

- Get property prices for the particular postcode by using the internet. Simply go to:
  http://www.landreg.gov.uk/propertyprice/interactive/ppr_ualbs.asp
  Then enter a postcode and you will immediately get details of the average price of different types of properties. For example, if you are buying a flat in postcode RG1 7NT, you will see that in the last three months 43 flats were sold in this postcode, and the average price was £149,881. This is a free service. You can also get this information by phone or email but you will be charged £10 (Telephone 01514736008, E-mail: enquiries.pic@landregistry.gov.uk).

- Why is this information useful?   Because if prices for similar properties are higher you know you will be able to find some good comparables.   If prices for similar properties are lower, you may have to reconsider *The Valuation Strategy* and instead apply *The Price Strategy*.

- Get comparables from 'Home Track' on the internet. Go to *http://www.hometrack.co.uk* (Tel 0800 019 4440) where you will be able to get a detailed market report for properties in any given postcode. The cost is about £15, and for that you get in-depth analysis of property, prices and trends, all focused on a particular postcode. You also get a list of nearby comparables and their locations, shown by dots on a street map.   So although you don't get the actual addresses of comparables, there is enough information for you to be able to go there and see the property and the address.   Naturally, you should be focused on the comparables with the highest values, and begin to compile a shortlist of three or four for giving to the Valuer.

- Once you have a few comparables, you may want to know the details of specific comparables. For instance, you may want to know the name of the owner, the actual price paid, the name of the Lender, and so on. To get this kind of information you can either knock on the front door and make enquiries, or you can get this information from the Land Registry. For a fee of just £2 you can get a copy of the Land Registry Entry for any given property in the UK, showing the legal history, price and date sold, full names of owners, etc. You can do this online by going to: *www.landregisteronline.gov.uk* and following the prompts to buy online.

Alternatively contact the Land Registry:
Telephone 0151 4736008
Fax 0151 4710151
Email: enquiries.pic@landregistry.gov.uk.

This is worth doing for the shortlist of two or three comparables that you will be giving to the Valuer – by giving the Valuer the full works (i.e. copies of the Land Registry entries) he won't have to double check the veracity of the information and he will be more inclined to go by the prices you give him.

Step three: Meet Valuer at property

- Make sure that you arrange to meet the Valuer at the property when he goes along to do the valuation. *This is critical. There is no other way of giving him the comparables.* Do this by stating on your mortgage application form that the Valuer must make an appointment with you, the Buyer, to gain access to the property. Then, when the Valuer contacts you to make an appointment, agree a date and time and make sure there will be no problems with the house occupants and gaining access on the day.

- Meet the Valuer at the property (be polite and friendly). Walk around with the Valuer, and offer to help in any way.

- Give The Valuer the comparables that you have prepared beforehand, and say *'to help you save time I have obtained some comparables which you can take with you'*. Remember two things: (i) The Valuer is working for the *Lender*, not for you, and (ii) he will use the PRICE given to him by the Lender and by you as a guide for arriving at a valuation figure. The Valuer will be trying hard to give a value that is equal to the PRICE rather than some other figure, provided the COMPARABLES stack up.

Using *The Valuation Strategy* for Selling Property

This strategy will enable a Seller to:

- Offer a property free of stamp duty as a means of attracting interest.

- Get a higher selling price than otherwise.

- Resolve a price impasse, whenever a Seller and Buyer cannot agree a price. Think of the strategy as a way of 'bridging the price gap' whenever a price cannot be agreed.

A Seller would only use this strategy when:

1. The Buyer and Seller cannot agree a price, or when a Buyer (for whatever reason) cannot pay the amount wanted by the Seller.

2. The Buyer is willing to agree a price but cannot afford the mortgage deposit or the buying costs (stamp duty, legal fees, etc).

This is a great strategy for Sellers even though the Seller is not involved in the Buyer's mortgage arrangements. However, the Seller needs to understand certain mortgage issues faced by the Buyer, to take full advantage of the strategy.

As mentioned earlier, when a PRICE is agreed between Buyer and Seller, this is the figure that goes on the Buyer's mortgage application form. And provided that the valuation carried out by the Lender is not *less* than the PRICE, the Buyer will usually get a mortgage based on this figure. To be clear then: **the loan amount is based on the SELLING PRICE, provided the VALUATION is not lower than the PRICE.**

TIP

As this book contains several strategies for avoiding stamp duty, you may feel overwhelmed with the amount of information. The best approach is to study each strategy separately, until all is clear, before going on to the next one. With confident understanding you can easily save a truly significant sum of money each time you buy or sell a property. Few other people will have the same advantage.

The strategy for the Seller is based on helping the Buyer get a mortgage based on a *higher* amount than the amount *actually paid* for the property. That way, the buyer ends up with 'cash in hand'.

So by helping the Buyer get a bigger mortgage than otherwise, this helps the Seller to sell a property more quickly and profitably.

This strategy is a 'win, win' situation for all concerned, and as you will see, it is a strategy that should be applied to virtually any property transaction, whether buying or selling.

How can the Seller help the Buyer get a bigger mortgage than otherwise? The strategy is based on the principle of getting a full market valuation for the property (the higher the valuation the better). A good (i.e. high) valuation will result in a more favourable loan for the Buyer, which in turn will benefit the Seller.

When a valuation is carried out this is the sequence of events:

1. The Buyer finds a property he wants to buy.

2. He agrees a price with the Seller.

3. The Seller and Buyer instruct solicitors.

4. The Buyer applies for a mortgage (and pays the mortgage company to carry out a valuation).

5. The mortgage company instructs a Valuer to carry out a valuation.

6. If the valuation is satisfactory (i.e. not lower than the PRICE) a mortgage is granted.

As mentioned, the Seller's objective is to help the Buyer get as high a valuation as possible so as to fully reflect the open market value of the property.

The following example explains the strategy further:

Example

- Seller's asking price: £230,000.

- Rock bottom amount that Seller is willing to accept after negotiation: £228,000.

- Buyer is only able to offer £224,000, so there is a £4,000 price gap that is preventing the sale from going ahead.

- For this example we assume a valuation of £238,000.

- Buyer can get a 95% Loan To Value mortgage.

- Deposit is therefore 5%.

In this example we will compare two scenarios from the point of view of a Seller:

Scenario one, based on the conventional sales approach

1. Original asking price: £230,000

2. Price reduction that Seller is willing to give: £228,000 (Buyer can only afford £224,000).

3. Selling price that would be agreed if Buyer were to proceed: £228,000

4. Amount that would be paid to Seller on completion if Buyer able to buy: £228,000.

5. Mortgage amount would be £216,600 (95% of £228,000).

6. Mortgage Deposit (payment from Buyer to Buyer's Lender) would be: £11,400 (5% of £228,000).

7. Buyer would have to pay for stamp duty, legal fees, mortgage valuation, and all other costs out of own resources as these cannot be included in the mortgage or property bank loan.

8. Property would be registered at the land registry with a value of £228,000.

9. In this scenario the sale would be lost unless the Seller or Buyer was willing to close the £4,000 price gap.

Scenario two based on The Valuation Strategy

1. Original asking price: £230,000

2. Price reduction that Seller is willing to give: £228,000 (Buyer can only afford £224,000).

3. Selling price agreed: £238,000 (£10,000 more than the amount to be paid for house).

4. Amount paid to Seller on completion: £238,000 (£10,000 more than the amount agreed for house).

5. Cash Incentive agreed (payment from Seller to Buyer): £10,000 (difference between £238,000 and £228,000, so Seller ends up getting £228,000 for house).

6. Mortgage amount is £226,100 (95% of £238,000).

7. Mortgage Deposit (payment from Buyer to Buyer's Lender): £11,900 (5% of £238,000).

8. Buyer can pay for stamp duty, legal fees, mortgage valuation, and all other costs from the £10,000 Cash Incentive, and still have money left over. Alternatively, it might be possible to use the Cash Incentive to finance the mortgage deposit (the Buyer may need to get a two- to three-day bridging loan if he has no savings).

9. Property is registered at the land registry with a value of £238,000.

10. In this scenario the sale goes through because the Seller ends up with £228,000 and the Buyer gets a £10,000 Cash Incentive (and is not short of money!).

We will now look at scenario two in more detail and explain the strategy further. What follows is a step-by-step procedure, including suggested dialogue.

STEP 1: Negotiate a price.

STEP 2: Make an offer.

STEP 3: Confirm it in writing.

STEP 1: Negotiate a price. The Buyer and Seller will negotiate a price in the conventional manner. It is assumed in this example that a price reduction of £2,000 was offered by the Seller but it could not be accepted. The Seller will now move onto STEP 2 and apply *The Valuation Strategy For Sellers* to bridge the price gap.

STEP 2: Make an offer. As the Seller is in danger of losing the opportunity to sell the house there is nothing to lose by making a special proposal to the Buyer. This proposal will enable the house to be sold at £228,000, plus giving the Buyer cash to pay for stamp duty and other legal costs. The dialogue would go along the lines that follow.

Dialogue:

- *'I have offered to reduce the price to £228,000 and you have told me that the maximum you can pay is £224,000. As we have a price gap of £4,000 I would like to make a special proposal that will help both of us in this situation. Can I explain this to you?'*

- *'Okay, what I would like to propose is that we agree on a selling price of £238,000. In this situation, you would get a mortgage based on £238,000, but you would only pay me £228,000. That would leave you with £10,000 cash in hand.'*

Note that you will have arrived at a figure of £238,000 having researched the values of similar properties in the area – more on this later.

- *'The price of £238,000 is the price that would go on all the paperwork including your mortgage application. This will help you to cover the costs you will incur in buying my house (legal fees, stamp duty, etc).'*

- *'In effect, you would be getting a mortgage or bank loan for £10,000 more than you need to buy this house. So on completion, your solicitor will give my solicitor the £238,000 as being the selling price for the house. Immediately afterwards, my solicitor will then give your solicitor a £10,000 Cash Incentive for giving to you. Of course, we will both need to tell our solicitors to do this, and I will confirm all of this in writing.'*

- *'The £10,000 price difference is called a 'Cash Incentive' and any experienced conveyancer will be familiar with this way of doing business. This £10,000 is a Cash Incentive from me to you but the money does not come from me – it comes from your own mortgage (from the money you are borrowing to buy my house).'*

At this point it is essential to make sure the Buyer understands how the Cash Incentive works. Explain that the Cash Incentive is a payment from the Buyer to himself. But the Cash Incentive money goes to the Buyer *via the Seller* as shown in the money flow diagram given earlier in this chapter.

To finish this point, explain that the cash incentive amounts to surplus money left over from the mortgage loan (the difference between the amount borrowed and the amount actually paid for the property). The Seller now continues the dialogue to finish the negotiations.

- *'Have a look at these advertisements. What I am proposing is no different to the way that large building companies operate, but on a smaller scale. In these advertisements, the building companies are selling direct to buyers, just as I am selling direct to you.'*

(Show advertisements depicting Cash Incentive offers from builders like Barratt. Answer any questions.)

- *'Let's summarize what you get out of the deal:*

  1. *You get to buy this house instead of losing it to another Buyer.*

  2. *You get £10,000 cash in hand for spending on anything you like. It could be used to pay for legal costs and stamp duty, and enable you to buy this house for little or no money down.*

  3. *You get to buy a property at below market value (a good bargain). This is so because you're buying a property valued at £238,000 but only paying £228,000.*

  4. *You get a property with equity, i.e. the potential profit that can be made when reselling the property. The equity is the difference between the market value and the amount owing on the property. For example, if you are getting a 95% mortgage on £238,000, you will owe £226,100. And if the market value is, say £238,000, the equity is £11,900.*

(Give the Buyer a separate sheet of paper with a list of the benefits. Answer any questions.)

- *'So can I take it that you agree in principle with this strategy? If so, I will give you some information for sending to your solicitor.'*

The benefits to the Buyer are:

1. Buyer is able to buy the property instead of losing it.

2. Buyer gets a property at below market value (a good bargain) because the amount actually paid for the property is less than the open market value.

3. Buyer gets a property with equity, i.e. the potential profit that can be made when reselling the property.

4. Buyer gets cash (in this example, £10,000) that can be used to pay for stamp duty, legal fees, conveyancing costs, or just be put into a savings account!).

The benefits to the Seller are:

1. Seller has found a Buyer and can sell the house.

2. Seller gets to sell the house at the required price (in this example a price gap of £4,000 has been bridged by the Buyer's own finance).

3. Seller's house is not devalued in the local market place (this can benefit the Seller if he/she owns other local properties, or has nearby relatives who own properties).

As already mentioned, the key point in this strategy is the price difference between the agreed selling price on which the mortgage is based and the actual amount paid to the Seller. This difference is known in the trade as a 'Cash Incentive' (not to be confused with a *'gifted deposit'*) and is common practice in the building industry. Ideally the cash incentive should not be more than 5% to 10% of the PRICE. If it is not over 5% (as in this example) it is more likely to be accepted by most Lenders. Note that cash incentives of 15% or more are not uncommon in the building industry.

Make sure the Buyer is aware that some Lenders do not allow Cash Incentives. He may, therefore, need to speak to a suitably qualified mortgage broker.

Note: The Buyer should always declare the *cash incentive* on his mortgage application form (there is nothing to hide). Most Lenders will usually not mind that the Buyer is getting a cash incentive provided the selling price is in line with the valuation report. Remember three things: (i) The *Cash Incentive* is not an additional loan from the Lender, (ii) the Lender is not involved with the cash incentive in any direct or legal sense, and (iii) Lenders themselves give cash incentives to Buyers (just look at any mortgage magazine).

To reassure the Buyer about this way of doing business, the Seller can explain that virtually all house building companies operate this way. Show the Buyer some typical examples of advertisements from house building companies.

Realize that you are using a perfectly ethical strategy often employed by building companies: you are 'giving' the Buyer a £10,000 Cash Incentive (for example) in return for buying your property. You are, in effect, enabling the Buyer to enjoy the same kind of benefits that building companies give to their clients.

Before putting the property up for sale, brief your solicitor about your intentions to offer a *Cash Incentive* to a Buyer, should you not be able to agree a price. Then, should the Buyer wish to, he can ask his solicitor to contact your solicitor to get confirmation that a Cash Incentive is a perfectly acceptable way of proceeding.

STEP 3: Confirm the deal in writing.

Let's recap. In step 1 you negotiated the best price possible in the usual manner but you were unable to agree a selling price with the Buyer. In step 2 you made an offer and got a positive response indicating co-operation with the strategy. Now, in step 3 you will be giving the Buyer two letters.

The first letter is a written confirmation from you to the Buyer to clarify the offer you have just made. This first letter would be issued in duplicate so that the Buyer can sign and return one copy to indicate an agreement in principle to proceed.

The second letter is a draft letter for the Buyer to send to his solicitor to get things moving. Both these letters are shown below, with suggested wording that can be adapted as necessary.

Note: These two letters would also be copied to any estate agent that may be involved in the transaction.

Price confirmation letter from Seller to Buyer

(date)

From: (Seller's name and address)

To: (Buyer's name and address)

Re: Sale of my property (enter property address)

Following our meeting, I confirm that we have agreed in principle the following price details for the sale of my house:

SELLING PRICE: **(Price agreed for selling property)**	*£ (enter agreed price)* *[Note: In the case of the above example, this would be £238,000]*
*Less Cash Incentive to buyer: **(For redecoration, repairs, and miscellaneous costs)**	*£ (enter agreed amount)* *[Note: In the case of the above example, this would be £10,000]*
Total cash on completion:	*£ (enter difference of above two figures)* *[Note: In the case of the above example, this would be £228,000]*

*The Cash Incentive referred to above is a sum of money that will be paid from the Seller's solicitor to the Buyer's solicitor on completion of the property transaction.

The address of my solicitor is as follows: (enter Seller's solicitor details).

I confirm that the Buyer will declare the cash incentive on his mortgage application form. (Delete this paragraph if Buyer is not using a loan to buy the property.)

It is understood that the sale of my house is subject to contract and a satisfactory valuation if it is being bought with a mortgage. The next step is to tell your solicitor to buy this property from me as detailed above.

[THE FOLLOWING PARAGRAPH APPLIES ONLY IF AN ESTATE AGENT IS INVOLVED]:

I confirm I will ask my estate agent to issue a 'memorandum of sale' and withdraw the property from the market. I will make clear to the estate agent that the SELLING PRICE is the higher amount (before deduction of the Cash Incentive). No discount applies to this transaction and the word 'discount' should not appear on any documentation as this would be incorrect. I will ask the estate agent to send a copy of the memorandum of sale to you so that you can ask your Lender to carry out the mortgage valuation of my property. Please sign the declaration below and give me a copy of this letter to indicate that you agree in principle to buy my property as explained above. I will then be able to withdraw the property from the market.

[THE FOLLOWING PARAGRAPH APPLIES ONLY IF AN ESTATE AGENT IS **NOT** INVOLVED]:

As no estate agent is involved in this transaction, this letter takes the place of the memorandum of sale. Please sign the declaration below and give me a copy of this letter to indicate that you agree in principle to buy my property as explained above. I will then be able to withdraw the property from the market.

If anything is not clear please contact me at any time.

Yours sincerely,

(enter Seller's name)

DECLARATION BY BUYER: *I agree in principle to BUY your property on the terms described above, subject to valuation and subject to contract.*

Signed: ....Date: ....

Print Name: ....

110

Letter from Buyer to Buyer's solicitor

Dear (Solicitor)

__Property:__ (Address)

I have asked you to act for me in the purchase of a property. I am now writing to explain that I wish to buy the above named property and the details are as follows:

1. *Name of Seller: (enter name).*

2. *Seller's solicitor: (enter name, address, and telephone number).*

3. *Price for buying property: (enter SELLING PRICE, not discounted amount).*

4. *Cash Incentive: I have also agreed to receive a Cash Incentive of £ (enter amount). This sum of money is to be paid to me upon completion, from the mortgage amount that I will be borrowing.*

I confirm that I will declare the cash incentive on my mortgage application form. (Delete this paragraph if Buyer is not using a loan to buy the property.)

Please find enclosed a copy of a price confirmation letter I have received from the Seller.

Yours sincerely

(name of Buyer)

The second letter, from the Buyer to his solicitor, is important as it will focus the Buyer's mind into taking the correct action and being committed to following the strategy.

If the Buyer will not sign the declaration in the letter there and then, you should allow the Buyer to take the letter away, and consult their solicitor should they wish to. In this event, you should make it clear that you cannot take the property off the market until the letter is signed or until you get a clear indication of an intention to buy.

Important Note: *When mentioning this strategy to a solicitor, only talk in terms of giving a Cash Incentive to the Buyer. Do not talk in terms of giving a cashback that is deducted from the Buyer's mortgage money, as this is not the case, and solicitors may regard this as somewhat dubious. Also, point out that the Buyer will be declaring the cash incentive on the mortgage application form, and that this is no different to the Cash Incentives given by house-building companies, a practice that is common all over the UK.*

To be absolutely clear, the Buyer will be using the *Lender's money* rather than the Buyer's own savings to pay for any price gap, for stamp duty and other costs. From the Buyer's point of view, in the above example, it is much better to end up with a mortgage of £226,100 and have £10,000 cash in hand, than to end up with a mortgage of £216,600 and no cash in hand.

The Buyer may end up paying a little more in monthly interest on a mortgage of £226,100 compared with £216,600, but the difference is relatively small compared with the advantage of having cash in hand. For example, if the mortgage interest is, say, 5% the monthly payment would be about £942 compared with £903 (a difference of about £39). And remember, the Buyer doesn't have to spend all of the Cash Incentive – he can, if he wants, put some of the Cash Incentive money into a high-interest savings account to offset the small increase in monthly interest.

A cash incentive can sometimes make or break a property deal. But do not let the Buyer get confused between a 'Cash Incentive' and a 'mortgage cashback'. The 'Cash Incentive' is what you, the Seller, offers him; the 'mortgage cashback' is completely different and is offered by the mortgage company. Of course, there is nothing to stop a Buyer getting both kinds of cashbacks in the same deal.

The Big Question for a Property Seller

We now come to the question: *How does a Seller get a full market valuation?* In the above example we need to get a valuation of £238,000 for this strategy to work. If the valuation carried out by the Lender is different to the PRICE what will happen?

If the VALUATION is *less than the PRICE*, the Lender will either say NO to the LOAN, or offer a reduced LOAN based on the lower VALUATION.

If the VALUATION is the *same as or higher than the PRICE*, the Lender will grant the LOAN applied for. Note that normally the Valuer will try to make the valuation match the PRICE, knowing that both the Lender and the Buyer want this.

For this strategy to work it is essential to get as high a valuation as possible, and not lower than the proposed PRICE. So how do you make sure that the Buyer gets the VALUATION that he needs for his mortgage? This is how:

Step one: check out local property prices

- Before offering the property for sale find out the approximate values of similar properties in the area. Do this by enquiring at local estate agents, by checking local property newspapers and by walking or driving around the area looking for other properties for sale or sold. This is the beginning of your research to find COMPARABLES.

TIP

Whenever you are out, in the local area, always be on the look-out for other properties being offered for sale or already sold (make a note of the addresses). Later, these addresses can prove very useful if you need comparables.

- If this initial research reveals several more highly priced properties that could be COMPARABLES, you know you may be able to apply *The Valuation Strategy For Sellers*. If you find that there are no similar properties at higher prices, or that the property you want to sell is not undervalued, you should consider not applying *The Valuation Strategy For Sellers.* If you find that comparable prices are *lower* rather than higher, you may have to reconsider the selling price or apply *The Price Strategy For Sellers* instead. Either way, your time will not be wasted.

Step two: Use the internet to get comparables.

- As mentioned earlier in this chapter you can get property prices for any particular postcode by using the internet. Simply go to *www.landreg.gov.uk* where you can get property prices for any part of the UK. .

  Why is this information useful for a Seller? Because if prices for similar properties are higher you know you will be able to find some good comparables.   If prices for similar properties are lower, you may have to reconsider whether it is feasible to use *The Valuation Strategy.* Instead, it may be better off applying *The Price Strategy.*

- Get comparables from 'Home Track' on the internet. Go to *www.hometrack.co.uk* (Tel 0800 019 4440) where you can get free price comparables for any postcode. Also, you will be able to get a detailed market report for properties in any given postcode for about £15. The objective here is to compile a shortlist of about three comparables for giving to the Valuer.

- Once you have a few comparables, you may want to know the details of specific comparables. For a fee of just £2 you can get a copy of the Land Registry Entry *for any given property* in the UK, online at *www.landregisteronline.gov.uk.* Alternatively contact the Land Registry:

  Telephone: 0151 473 6008
  Fax: 0151 471 0151
  Email: enquiries.pic@landregistry.gov.uk.

  This is worth doing for the shortlist of two or three comparables that you will be giving to the Valuer.

Step three: Meet Valuer at property

- Clearly if you are selling your home *you* are likely to be the person to meet the Valuer. In any event it is important to make sure that *you* arrange to meet the Valuer at the property when he goes along to do the valuation. *This is critical. There is no other way of giving him the comparables.* Do this by telling the Buyer to state on his mortgage application form that the Valuer must make an appointment with you personally (the Seller) to gain access to the property.

- Meet the Valuer at the property.

- Give the Valuer the comparables that you have prepared beforehand.

Summary of *The Valuation Strategy* (for buyers)

1. Brief your solicitor about the use of a 'Cash Incentive' to buy your next property. Say that you will be asking the Seller to give you a small Cash Incentive upon completion. Should you need to explain further, go through the two scenarios explained in this chapter. You should not need to explain the whole strategy. If the solicitor is not familiar with the concept of a cash incentive in a property transaction find another solicitor. The purpose here is to 'prime' your solicitor to be receptive and to fully co-operate with the Seller's solicitor when the time comes. Any experienced conveyancer will be familiar with the concept of a Cash Incentive.

2. Find a mortgage broker who can find you the best possible mortgage which will allow a Cash Incentive from the Seller

3. Find a property and negotiate the best price reduction possible. Having clearly ascertained the lowest price you can get, go on to ask the Seller to sell the house to you at the full value price. Explain that the difference between the full value price and the negotiated price represents the Cash Incentive that you will get. Since the Seller is not financially affected, there should be no objections.

4. Offer the Seller an additional £300 (or some other amount) to encourage co-operation. Do this by offering to buy a low-value item in the property for £300, and say this will be a separate cash transaction between you and the Seller.

5. Show the Seller one or more advertisements used by well known building companies who offer Cash Incentives in the form of stamp duty payments, and so on. Explain that what you are proposing is no different to the way that large building companies operate, but on a smaller scale. Explain that a Cash Incentive in the building industry is a perfectly legal and common way of doing business.

6. Tell the Seller the next step is to inform their solicitor (and estate agent if applicable). Do this by using the sample letters given.

7. Make sure you enter the agreed full market value PRICE on the mortgage application form, and clearly state that the Valuer must contact you personally to arrange to see the property for the VALUATION (do not give alternative contact details for the Valuer). It is crucial that you are able to meet the Valuer at the property because this is the only opportunity you have for giving him the COMPARABLES.

8. Find out the highest value comparables in the area by doing research in the locality and on the internet, and prepare a shortlist of two or three comparables for giving to the Valuer (as a rule the Valuer needs three comparables).

9. Follow through with all parties (Seller, Estate Agent, Solicitor, Lender) to get things moving.

Summary of *The Valuation Strategy* (for sellers)

1. Brief your solicitor about the use of a 'Cash Incentive' to sell your property. Say that you will be asking the Buyer to accept a small Cash Incentive. By all means explain the strategy to the Solicitor, but you should not need to.

2. Prepare a list of local COMPARABLES so that you can be ready to apply *The Valuation Strategy* should it be necessary. Use the highest valued comparables in the area by doing research in

the locality and on the internet, and prepare a shortlist of three.

3. Get full Land Registry copies of the selected COMPARABLES if you will be giving them to the Valuer.

4. Prepare copies of advertisements used by national building companies showing Cash Incentives and explain to the Buyer that what you are proposing is no different.

5. Prepare the Buyer Benefits sheet to help Buyer understand the strategy.

6. Use this strategy only if the Buyer is not able or willing to pay the minimum SELLING PRICE you require. Then apply *The Valuation Strategy* exactly as explained in this chapter, taking care to ensure that the Buyer understands how the Cash Incentive works.

7. Before finishing the negotiations, tell the Buyer the next step is to inform his solicitor (and estate agent if applicable). Do this by using the sample letters given above.

8. Tell Buyer to enter the agreed full market value as the SELLING PRICE on the mortgage application form, and clearly state that the Valuer must contact you personally (the Seller) to arrange to see the property for the VALUATION – no alternative contacts must be given to the Valuer. It is crucial that you are able to meet the Valuer at the property because this is the only opportunity you have if you are going to give him the COMPARABLES.

9. Follow through with all parties (Buyer, Estate Agent, and Solicitor) to get things moving.

The Combination Strategy

So far we have looked at the following six strategies:

1	**The Tax Exemption Strategy**
2	**The Threshold Strategy**
3	**The Link Strategy**
4	**The Mortgage Cashback Strategy**
5	**The Price Strategy**
6	**The Valuation Strategy**

The Combination Strategy is a way of exploiting any 'mix and match' of these six strategies to give a powerful and virtually infallible way of avoiding, reducing or saving the cost of stamp duty.

Every time you buy a property you will be using a different mix of these strategies, depending on the circumstances. Furthermore, it is unlikely that you will be using just one of these strategies whenever buying a property.

So let's look at how you may combine these strategies and make the best savings possible. (Clearly, it will help your understanding if you first read the preceding chapters before continuing).

The Tax Exemption Strategy, based on getting tax relief in disadvantaged areas, is a clear-cut situation: it either applies or does not apply. If it does apply, then it would be used in conjunction with other strategies in this book.

The Threshold Strategy, based on exploiting stamp duty thresholds and negotiating lower property prices, should always be considered if the asking PRICE is near to or within the price threshold. For example, if the property is priced at, say, £269,000 you know that the price has not been reduced to get under any particular threshold. In these circumstances you would dismiss *The Threshold Strategy* and consider another strategy.

However, if the property is priced at, say, £259,000 or £262,000 you know that either A or B is a possibility:

A. The owner considered the property was worth around, say, £255,000, but as this is too close to the stamp duty threshold it wouldn't attract buyers. Therefore, in order to attract buyers the price was changed upwards to £259,000. This gives room for negotiation.

B. The owner considered the property was worth around, say, £255,000, but as this is too close to the stamp duty threshold it wouldn't attract buyers. Therefore, in order to attract buyers the price was changed downwards to £250,000. This will stop buyers being put off by the stamp duty threshold (the jump from 1% to 3%), but clearly the price is unlikely to be reduced further.

So *The Threshold Strategy* is a pretty clear cut situation: it either applies or it's a non-starter (you won't know until you negotiate). If there is a possibility the strategy may apply (because the price is near the threshold) see what other strategies in this book it can be combined with *before* you approach the Seller.

The Link Strategy, based on avoiding a punitive rate of stamp duty when buying more than one property from the same Seller, can be combined with just about any other strategy in this book. You would, of course, only consider using this strategy if there was a possibility of buying a property from a Seller that has already sold you a property in the past (or if buying two or more properties from anybody).

Looking at other strategies, you could get a £1,000 cashback mortgage from a Lender using *The Mortgage Cashback Strategy*, and on top of that you could get a £3,000 Cash Incentive from the Seller based on *The Valuation Strategy*. So, in this example you have combined several strategies to give you a big saving in stamp duty, plus £4,000 in cash.

The point is this: whatever property deal you may be orchestrating, exploit all six strategies in whichever ways are possible. Some property deals may warrant all six strategies! Others may just warrant one of the strategies. Most property deals will be amenable to at least two of the strategies. It would be very unusual to buy a property without being able to apply at least one of the stamp duty planning strategies in this book.

The Mortgage Cashback Strategy, based on getting a cashback from the Lender, is great provided you are not sacrificing some other useful feature of the mortgage package. This strategy would be used in conjunction with any other strategy that may apply, to give you additional funds for paying stamp duty and other costs. Do not dismiss this strategy just because you are also getting a Cash Incentive from the Seller or mortgage broker. Get as many Cash Incentives as you can, from all directions!

We now come to the ideal *combination strategy method* to give a virtually foolproof way of saving money to pay for stamp duty (see Fig. 8).

Fig. 8 - The Combination Strategy
(Combination of Valuation and Price strategies)

The Valuation Strategy ▶	This strategy is based on the Buyer obtaining (and the Seller giving) a Cash Incentive that is related to the VALUATION of the property, and will apply whenever prices of comparable properties are higher. **Use this strategy when the price reduction negotiated is nil or not sufficient *and* prices of COMPARABLES are higher.** (If price is the same or lower, use *The Price Strategy* without *The Valuation Strategy.)*
The Price Strategy ▶	This strategy is based on the Buyer obtaining (and the Seller giving) a Cash Incentive that is equivalent to the price reduction the Seller is willing to give, and will apply whenever ***The Valuation Strategy*** cannot be used. **Use this strategy when price reduction is nil or not sufficient *and* prices of COMPARABLES are the same or lower.** (If prices of comparables are higher, use *The Valuation Strategy with or without The Price Strategy.)*

Fig 8 shows when to use these strategies, so that *whatever the comparables* we still have a viable strategy for getting a significant Cash Incentive and overcoming a property price that is too high.

Combining these two strategies is at the heart of stamp duty planning, and to thoroughly appreciate how this works several examples follow. Study these examples carefully as they show how the strategy works in practice and how powerful it can be.

121

Example 1.

1. Asking price for apartment is £150,000.

2. Price is negotiated down to £148,000.

3. Using *The Price Strategy* you could ask the Seller to agree to a £2,000 Cash Incentive. But prior to negotiating the deal you checked the COMPARABLES and established that the best similar apartments nearby have sold at about £155,000.

4. Since the COMPARABLES are higher than the asking price of £150,000 you decide to use *The Valuation Strategy*. So you go on to ask for a £7,000 Cash Incentive. Note that £7,000 is the total of the price reduction (£2,000) and the COMPARABLES (on average £5,000 higher).

5. If the COMPARABLES had been about the same or lower than the asking price, you would have used *The Price Strategy* and just asked for a £2,000 Cash Incentive. However, in this scenario you would have added the cost of stamp duty to the asking price (say £1,500), giving you a Cash Incentive of £3,500.

6. Naturally, you would also use any of the other strategies that may apply.

Example 2.

1. Asking price for apartment is £150,000.

2. Price is negotiated down to £146,000.

3. Using *The Price Strategy* you could ask the Seller to agree to a £4,000 Cash Incentive. But prior to negotiating the deal you checked the COMPARABLES and established that the best similar apartments nearby have sold at about £150,000.

4. Since the COMPARABLES are similar to the asking price of £150,000 you decide to use *The Price Strategy*. So you consider asking for a £4,000 Cash Incentive. Note that no Cash Incentive for the COMPARABLES can be realized because they are similar in price to the property you are buying.

5. If the COMPARABLES had been higher than the asking price, you would have used *The Valuation Strategy*.

6. Since you are using *The Price Strategy* you decide to combine the discount amount with the stamp duty amount and ask for a Cash Incentive of £5,500 (total of £4,000 discount plus £1,500 stamp duty). If this is not clear you should re-read *The Price Strategy*.

7. Naturally, you would also use any of the other strategies that may apply.

Example 3.

1. Asking price for apartment is £150,000.

2. The COMPARABLES are similar in price.

3. A tiny price reduction of £500 is negotiated, bringing the payment amount down to 149,500. You risk losing the property if you don't agree to go ahead.

4. However, the house has a conservatory, whereas the three COMPARABLES that have been short listed do not have conservatories. This is a 'unique feature' and it puts the value of the target property up by £3,000 in relation to the comparables (remember that you must point this out to the Valuer when you meet him).

5. Note that if the target property had, for example, a bigger garden than the COMPARABLES the same principles apply. *Anything* that increases the value of the target property (compared to the COMPARABLES) can be used to increase the valuation – the higher the valuation, the bigger the Cash Incentive.

6. Using *The Valuation Strategy* you agree a selling PRICE of £153,000 with a Cash Incentive of £3,500, giving the Seller a net amount of £149,500. Note that the £3,500 Cash Incentive is the total of the price reduction (£500) and the price difference of £3,000 (COMPARABLES at £150,000 and the target property plus conservatory at £153,000).

7. In this example you have combined *The Price Strategy* and *The Valuation Strategy* to get a Cash Incentive of £3,500. But note that you would only ever present one of these strategies to the Seller (otherwise everybody would get confused!). Also, note that as soon as you realized you could use the conservatory to get a higher valuation, you knew that you would only be presenting *The Valuation Strategy* to the Seller.

8. Naturally, you would also use any of the other strategies that may apply.

Example 4.

1. Asking price for apartment is £150,000.

2. The COMPARABLES are similar in price.

3. A big price reduction of £5,000 is negotiated, as some renovation work is required, bringing the payment amount down to £145,000.

4. The house has a converted second toilet under the stairs, so you check the COMPARABLES and discover the following:

    a. COMPARABLE one has no second toilet and was sold for £149,000.

    b. COMPARABLE two has no second toilet and was sold for £148,000.

    c. COMPARABLE three has a second toilet and was sold for £152,000.

5. You decide to use all three COMPARABLES and you will tell the Valuer that as the property you are buying has a converted second toilet the value is about £152,000 (same as comparable number 3).

6. You know straight away that you will only be using *The Valuation Strategy* with the Seller because you are going for a valuation that is greater than the asking price of the target property. So you will be agreeing a PRICE of £152,000 with a Cash Incentive of £7,000. Note that £7,000 is the total of the price reduction (£5,000) and the valuation price difference of

£2,000 (the COMPARABLE with the second toilet is on average £2,000 higher than the asking price of £150,000).

7. In this example you have combined *The Price Strategy* and *The Valuation Strategy* to get a Cash Incentive of £7,000. But note that you would only ever present one of these strategies to the Seller (otherwise everybody gets confused!). Also, note that as soon as you realized you could use the converted toilet to get a higher valuation, you knew that you would only be presenting *The Valuation Strategy* to the Seller, even though the price reduction was *greater* than the valuation difference.

8. Naturally, you would also use any of the other strategies that may apply.

Example 5.

1. A house is for sale at £230,000. The Buyer knows he is able to get a 95% mortgage but has little money for the 5% deposit. So he offers £221,000 as this would reduce the amount of deposit he would have to pay the Lender.

2. After negotiations, the Seller comes down to £226,000 and will not reduce the price any further. There is a real risk that the Buyer will lose the house as there is a price gap of £4,000.

3. To resolve the problem the Buyer decides to ask the Seller for a £9,000 Cash Incentive by combining *The Valuation Strategy* and *The Price Strategy*.

4. Let's recap the situation so far in this example: The asking price was £230,000 and the Buyer offered £221,000 but this was rejected. The best reduction offered by the Seller was £226,000 (a price reduction of £4,000). The buyer is keen to get the property but does not have enough money for the 5% deposit so he decides to ask the Seller for a £9,000 Cash Incentive. The table on the next page summarizes the possible scenarios.

Example 5 - Cash Incentive Request

	A (£) Advertised price	B (£) Buyer's offer	C (£) Seller's minimum price	D (£) Buyer's proposal
Selling price	230,000	221,000	226,000	235,000
Cash-incentive	Not applicable	Not applicable	Not applicable	9,000
Net amount received by seller	230,000	221,000 (cannot be accepted)	226,000	226,000
Buyer's loan based on 95% mortgage	218,500	209,950	214,700	223,250
Buyer's deposit based on 5%	11,500	11,050	11,300	11,750
Less Cash Incentive	none	None	None	9,000
Amount required for deposit	11,500	11,050	11,300	2,750

Column A is the original price advertised by the Seller. Column B is the best 'conventional' offer the Buyer can make in the hope of reducing the deposit. This offer cannot be accepted by the Seller, but even if it were accepted the deposit amount would only be reduced by £450!

Column C shows the best offer the Seller is willing to accept. This would leave the Buyer with a deposit of £11,300 instead of £11,500 (still too much). Column D shows the proposal made by the Buyer to secure the house and give the Seller a deal he will accept.

Reading from left to right in the bottom row you can see that the deposit amount does not vary significantly until you get to the Cash Incentive deal which has a direct impact on the deposit.

Clearly, if using a Cash Incentive to finance a mortgage deposit, a Buyer may have to obtain a bridging loan for two or three days (the time interval between paying the deposit to the solicitor to complete the deal and receiving the Cash Incentive to repay the bridging loan).

Most people are held back from buying a property because of the deposit required by the mortgage company. They try to resolve this by negotiating a lower price. But note that any reduction in price has an insignificant effect on the deposit.

The solution, in this example, is to combine *The Valuation Strategy* with *The Discount Strategy* and get a big Cash Incentive of £9,000. Only *The Valuation Strategy* would be presented to the Seller. Naturally, the Buyer will have done his homework and established that getting a valuation of £235,000 is feasible.

The £9,000 Cash Incentive is the total of the £4,000 price reduction plus the £5,000 price increase. So the selling price is £235,000 and the mortgage is based on this figure. The money for the £9,000 Cash Incentive is money left over from the mortgage loan, given that the actual amount paid for the house is £226,000. To be clear: The mortgage company gives £235,000 to the Seller, but as the Seller has agreed to accept only £226,000, he returns £9,000 to the Buyer in the form of a Cash Incentive.

In this example the Seller is happy as he gets the minimum of £226,000 he wanted. The Buyer is happy as he did not lose the house and only had to pay £2,750 deposit instead of £11,750. Of course, against this the Buyer has a slightly bigger mortgage to pay off. But the extra interest is very small compared with the advantages of gaining a valuable property asset and paying a much smaller deposit.

This solution has given the Buyer a home and saved him much more than the cost of stamp duty. It has also enabled the Seller to get a successful sale, and the Lender to get a new client. Even the tax authorities are happy as they get paid stamp duty on a higher SELLING PRICE. Everybody wins!

Using the *Combination Strategy* for Property Sellers

As with buyers, the *Combination Strategy* can be used by sellers to great advantage. You do this by exploiting any 'mix and match' of the strategies in this book. In particular the five main strategies give a powerful way of avoiding or reducing the cost of stamp duty as a way of attracting buyer interest, achieving a successful sale, and getting a good price.

Here are the main strategies that can be combined to make a property sale as successful as possible:

The Tax Exemption Strategy, based on getting tax relief in a disadvantaged area or by virtue of the property being classified as belonging to charity, is a clear-cut situation: the tax exemption either applies or does not apply. If it does apply, then it would be used in conjunction with other strategies in this book.

The Threshold Strategy, based on exploiting stamp duty thresholds, should always be considered if the asking PRICE is near to or within the price threshold. For example, if you think your property is worth about £250,000, you need to price it at less than £251,000 or more than £260,000 to attract interest.

If offering the property at a price between £250,000 and £270,000, it should ideally be offered free of stamp duty, and if you don't get the asking price you could apply *The Price Strategy* or *The Valuation Strategy*.

The Link Strategy, based on avoiding a punitive rate of stamp duty when buying more than one property from the same Seller, can be combined with just about any other strategy in this book.

The point is this: whatever property deal you may be orchestrating, exploit any and all of the strategies in whichever ways are possible.

As already mentioned in this chapter, the most powerful *Combination Strategy* involves a combination of the *Price Strategy* and the *Valuation Strategy* as summarized in the table that follows on the next page.

Using *The Combination Strategy* for Selling Property

As a Seller you can apply any combination of the Valuation and Price strategies to great effect.

128

You will appreciate that, *whatever the comparables,* the Seller will always have a viable strategy for proposing to a potential Buyer. If the comparables are higher than the proposed selling price use *The Valuation Strategy.* If the comparables are the same or lower, use *The Price Strategy.* Naturally, you would hold these strategies 'up your sleeve' and only bring them out if a Buyer is not willing to pay the price you need. Think of these strategies as ways of bridging a price gap in your negotiations.

Whenever a Seller is thinking of selling a property he should in all situations first check the local comparables.

As mentioned, combining these two strategies is at the heart of stamp duty planning. To fully appreciate how this works have a read through the examples below. Study these examples carefully as they show how powerful this strategy can be.

Example 1.

1. Asking price for apartment is £150,000.

2. Price is negotiated down to £148,000 but it is not enough to satisfy the Buyer.

3. Using *The Price Strategy* you could offer the Buyer a £2,000 Cash Incentive (so Seller would get £148,000 and Buyer would get a £2,000 Cash Incentive). But prior to negotiating the deal you checked the COMPARABLES and established that the best similar apartments nearby have sold at about £155,000.

4. Since the COMPARABLES are higher than your asking price of £150,000 you decide to use *The Valuation Strategy.* So you offer the Buyer a £7,000 Cash Incentive. Note that £7,000 is the total of the price reduction (£2,000) and the COMPARABLES (on average £5,000 higher). So Seller gets £148,000 and Buyer gets a £7,000 Cash Incentive. The selling price would be registered at £155,000. This is how you *combine* the two strategies.

5. If the COMPARABLES had been about the same or lower than the asking price, you would have used *The Price Strategy* and just offered a £2,000 Cash Incentive.

6. Naturally, you would also use any of the other strategies that may apply.

Example 2.

1. Asking price for apartment is £150,000.

2. Price is negotiated down to £146,000 but it is not enough to satisfy the Buyer.

3. Using *The Price Strategy* you could offer the Buyer a £4,000 Cash Incentive (so Seller would get £146,000 and Buyer would get a £4,000 Cash Incentive). But prior to negotiating the deal you checked the COMPARABLES and established that the best similar apartments nearby have sold at about £150,000.

4. Since the COMPARABLES are similar to the asking price of £150,000 you decide to use *The Price Strategy*. So you offer the Buyer a £4,000 Cash Incentive. Note that no Cash Incentive for the COMPARABLES can be realized because they are similar in price to the property you are selling. The selling price is registered at £150,000.

5. If the COMPARABLES had been higher than your proposed selling price, you would have used *The Valuation Strategy*.

6. Naturally, you would also use any of the other strategies that may apply.

Example 3.

1. Asking price for apartment is £150,000.

2. Price is negotiated down to £149,500. Although this price reduction is small, the Seller simply does not want to reduce it any further. Unfortunately it is not enough to satisfy the Buyer.

3. The COMPARABLES are similar in price.

4. However, the house has a conservatory, whereas the three COMPARABLES that have been short-listed do not have conservatories. This is a 'unique feature' and it puts the value

130

of your property up by £3,000 in relation to the comparables (remember that you must point this out to the Valuer when you meet him).

5. Note that if your property had, for example, a bigger garden than the COMPARABLES the same principles apply. *Anything that increases the value of your property (compared to the COMPARABLES) can be used to increase the valuation* – the higher the valuation, the bigger the Cash Incentive.

6. Using *The Valuation Strategy* you agree a selling PRICE of £153,000 with a Cash Incentive of £3,500, giving the Seller a net amount of £149,500. Note that the £3,500 Cash Incentive is the total of the price reduction (£500) and the price difference of £3,000 (COMPARABLES at £150,000 and the target property plus conservatory at £153,000). The selling price would be registered at £153,000.

7. In this example you have combined *The Price Strategy* and *The Valuation Strategy* to give the Buyer a Cash Incentive of £3,500. But note that you would only ever present one of these strategies to the Buyer (otherwise everybody gets confused!). Also, note that as soon as you realized you could use the conservatory to get a higher valuation, you knew that you would only be presenting *The Valuation Strategy* to the Buyer.

8. Naturally, you would also use any of the other strategies that may apply.

Example 4.

1. Asking price for apartment is £150,000.

2. A big price reduction is negotiated down to £145,000 (as the kitchen needs modernizing) but it is not enough to satisfy the Buyer, who only wants to pay £140,000.

3. The COMPARABLES are similar in price.

4. The house has a converted second toilet under the stairs, so you check the COMPARABLES and discover the following:

   a. COMPARABLE one has no second toilet and was sold for 149,000.

b.   COMPARABLE two has no second toilet and was sold for £148,000.

c.   COMPARABLE three has a second toilet and was sold for £152,000.

5.   You decide to use all three COMPARABLES and you will tell the Valuer that as your property *has a converted second toilet* the value is about £152,000 (same as COMPARABLE 'C').

6.   You know straight away that you will only be using *The Valuation Strategy* to bridge the price gap with the Buyer because you are going for a valuation that is greater than your asking price of £150,000. So you will be agreeing a PRICE of £152,000 with a Cash Incentive of £7,000. Note that £7,000 is the total of the price reduction (£5,000) and the valuation price difference of £2,000 (the COMPARABLE with the second toilet is on average £2,000 higher than the asking price of £150,000).

7.   In this example you have combined *The Price Strategy For Sellers* and *The Valuation Strategy For Sellers* to offer a £7,000 Cash Incentive to bridge a price gap of £5,000. But note that you would only ever present one of these strategies to the Buyer (otherwise everybody gets confused!). Also, note that as soon as you realized you could use the converted toilet to get a higher valuation, you knew that you would be presenting *The Valuation Strategy For Sellers* to the Buyer, even though the price reduction was *greater* than the valuation difference.

8.   Naturally, you would also use any of the other strategies that may apply.

Example 5.

1.   The Seller offers to sell his house at £230,000 plus a £4,000 Cash Incentive. This means the Buyer gets £4,000 on completion which he can use to pay for stamp duty, legal fees, deposit or anything else. The Seller would get a net £226,000 which is the minimum amount acceptable.

2.   A Buyer is able to get a 95% mortgage but has little money for the 5% deposit. So the Buyer offers £225,000 but still wants the same £4,000 Cash Incentive.

3. The Seller says this would give him a net £221,000 which is not enough, and the minimum he can accept is £226,000. So the Seller offers the Buyer a solution based on a £9,000 Cash Incentive (see column C in the table below).

Example 5 – cash incentive

	A (£) Advertised offer	B (£) Buyer's offer	C (£) Seller's proposal
Selling price	230,000	225,000	235,000
Cash Incentive	4,000	4,000	9,000
Net amount received by seller	226,000	221,000	226,000
Buyer's loan based on 95% mortgage	218,500	213,750	223,250
Buyer's deposit based on 5%	11,500	11,250	11,750
Less Cash Incentive	4,000	4,000	9,000
Amount required for deposit	7,500	7,250	2,750

Column A is the original price advertised by the Seller. Column B is the offer made by the Buyer which cannot be accepted as the Seller wants a minimum of £226,000. Column C is the counter-offer made by the Seller to secure a sale.

The Buyer offered a lower price (£225,000) in the hope of reducing the amount required for his deposit - this is the 'conventional' approach made by most people. The table above shows that paying £5,000 less (col. B) will only reduce the deposit by £250, an insignificant amount!

The Seller is keen to sell the house so he uses *The Valuation Strategy* to agree a SELLING PRICE of £235,000, and he combines this with *The Price Strategy* to give a big Cash Incentive of £9,000.

In this example the Seller is happy as he gets the minimum of £226,000 he wanted. The Buyer is happy as he did not lose the house and only had to pay £2,750 deposit instead of £11,750. Of course, against this the Buyer has a slightly bigger mortgage to pay off. But the extra interest is very small compared to the advantages of gaining a valuable property asset, paying a much smaller deposit, and not losing the property to another buyer.

This solution has saved the Buyer much more than the cost of stamp duty and it has enabled the Seller to get a successful sale. Even the tax authorities are happy as they get paid stamp duty on a higher SELLING PRICE. Everybody wins!

Summary of *The Combination Strategy* for buying property:

1. Study all the strategies for avoiding stamp duty and use those that best apply to your particular property deal.

2. Take advantage of Cash Incentives from the Seller, the Lender, and the Mortgage Broker, whenever possible. There is no reason why several Cash Incentives cannot be applied to the same property transaction.

3. Do your homework before negotiating with the Seller: check out the COMPARABLES as you need to know these for applying *The Price Strategy* or *The Valuation Strategy*.

4. Use low-priced COMPARABLES to help you negotiate a price reduction in the conventional manner. Use high-priced COMPARABLES to help you get a high valuation from the Valuer.

5. Get a *Cash Incentive* whether COMPARABLES are higher, lower, or similar to the property you are buying. Do this by using both *The Price Strategy* and *The Valuation Strategy* but only present one of these strategies to the Seller.

6. Get a *Cash Incentive* whether or not a lower price can be negotiated. Do this by using both *The Price Strategy* and *The Valuation Strategy* but only present one of these strategies to the Seller.

Summary of *The Combination Strategy* for selling property:

1. Study all the strategies for avoiding stamp duty and use those that best apply to your particular property deal.

2. Offer the property 'free of stamp duty' or 'stamp duty paid' as a way of getting a better market response. Also consider offering a Cash Incentive alongside the asking price.

3. Do your homework before putting the property up for sale: check out the COMPARABLES to decide whether to use *The Price Strategy* or *The Valuation Strategy*. Remember to combine these two strategies, but present only one of these strategies when negotiating.

4. Use high-priced COMPARABLES and/or unique property features to help get a high valuation from the Valuer.

5. Offer the Buyer as big a Cash Incentive as possible (ideally about 5% of the selling price, but not more than 10%) as a way of getting a sale and a good price.

*****

PART TWO

Other Stamp Duty Planning Strategies Including Commercial Property

Introduction to PART TWO

The first three strategies that follow apply to residential and non-residential property. Strategy number four onwards is mainly focused on non-residential property such as land and commercial property. PART TWO finishes with a chapter dedicated to a selection of the best ways to get on the property ladder.

The reader is urged to read PART ONE of this book before proceeding any further, as this will aid comprehension of what follows.

Here is a list of the strategies covered in this section of this book:

1. The Gift Strategy

2. The Company Strategy

3. The Back-to-Back Strategy

4. The Threshold Strategy For Non-Residential Property

5. The Link Strategy For Non-Residential Property

6. The Land Strategy For Non-Residential Property

7. The Price Strategy For Non-Residential Property

8. The Valuation Strategy For Non-Residential Property

9. The Combination Strategy For Non-Residential Property

10. Top 10 Ways to Get on the Property Ladder

The Gift Strategy

When you buy a property you pay stamp duty. But when you receive a property as a *gift* stamp duty does not usually apply.

It would be illegal to make a property gift and then receive a hidden, secret or indirect payment for the property without paying stamp duty. Gifting a property to anybody is perfectly legal provided that, if and when payment is received, the appropriate stamp duty is paid.

However, there are circumstances when stamp duty can be legally avoided by making use of the gift exemption, so let's look at the possibilities.

Stamp duty is only payable when there is a transfer of ownership *and when* a payment is made for the property. But what is the situation when there is a transfer of ownership and no payment is made?

Answer: No stamp duty is liable. So if John makes a gift of a house to Mary, neither party has to pay stamp duty, regardless of the value of the house and regardless of the relationship between the two people.

The tax authorities do not care whether the gift is between close family members or between strangers, it makes no difference. But they do care about *reciprocity: there must be no reciprocal payment.* The gift must be genuine in the sense that there must be no 'consideration'. That is, there must be no financial payment or payment in kind.

But suppose two people give a property to each other as a gift, i.e. they swap or exchange properties. Do they both pay stamp duty? The answer is YES because the tax authorities do not recognize the verb *swap* or *exchange* when it comes to stamp duty. When you exchange properties you are buying a property from each other (instead of paying money, you are using your property to make a payment in kind).

Here are some examples of what you can and cannot do when it comes to gifts, and how you can avoid stamp duty by using *The Gift Strategy*.

Example 1.

John owns a house worth £270,000. Peter owns a bungalow worth £200,000. They want to exchange properties. If they exchange properties at these prices Peter will have to pay John £70,000 (the price difference between the two properties).

The deal goes ahead, and Peter has to pay stamp duty based on 3% of £270,000 (£8,100). John has to pay stamp duty based on 1% of £200,000 (£2,000). Total stamp duty: £10,100.

Alternative scenario for example 1:

John and Peter may have *thought* about swapping properties and about various pricing possibilities but nothing has been agreed or put in writing (so the *selling prices have not yet been established*). Thus there is no collusion, and after all, they are free to think whatever they like!

Peter and John each decide to advertise their houses for sale at £250,000 and £180,000. They do this in their own separate ways, at different times. This is perfectly legitimate. Among the responses that Peter gets, he decides to contact John. Among the responses that John gets he decides to contact Peter.

Peter decides to accept the advertised offer from John. Later John decides to accept the advertised offer from Peter. John decides to sell his house to Peter for £250,000. And Peter decides to sell his house to John for £180,000. Note that no prices have been *reduced* as a way of avoiding stamp duty – this would be illegal.

The deal goes ahead, and Peter has to pay stamp duty based on 1% of £250,000 (£2,500). John has to pay stamp duty based on 1% of £180,000 (£1,800). Total stamp duty: £4,300 (a big saving of £5,800 compared with the previous scenario!).

In this example three points come to mind:

1. It is perfectly legal to sell a property at any price you like. You can, if you like, sell a house for just £10 and the Buyer would pay no stamp duty. However, *there must be no reciprocity*, i.e. no additional cash payment or payment in kind. If there is a reciprocal payment then stamp duty will apply on the total consideration paid or on the open market value of the property.

2. In the above alternative scenario, note that no price reductions were made by either party. John has not reduced the price of his house from £270,000 to £250,000 as a way of avoiding stamp duty (this would be illegal). There are no records to show that John (or his estate agent) has advertised the house for £270,000, and therefore nobody (including the tax authorities) can say that John has reduced the price to £250,000. Equally, there are no records to show that Peter has reduced his price from £200,000 to £180,000. Hence, there has been no reciprocity – just two separate property purchase transactions. In this example, John and Peter were careful to keep separate each property transaction and not making any reference to *swapping* or *exchange*.

3. The key here is to not be accused of swapping properties at a lower market value as a way of avoiding stamp duty. Since no selling price was set and then discounted, there can be no accusations. And provided there is no reciprocity or undeclared payment, the market value of each property becomes irrelevant.

Example 2.

Mother buys a flat in her own name and then gives it to her daughter as a gift. Stamp duty applies when flat purchased by mother. But when the flat is given to daughter as a *gift* no stamp duty applies because there was no consideration.

Example 3.

Mother gives money to daughter as a gift and daughter buys flat in her own name. Stamp duty applies when daughter purchased flat.

Example 4.

John gives his house to Mary as a gift. No stamp duty applies as there was no consideration. A few months later, Mary buys British Airways shares worth £200,000 and gives them as a Christmas present to John. This would be regarded as a payment in kind and stamp duty would be liable on £200,000.

Example 5.

John wants to sell his house to Mary. The market value is £270,000. John decides to sell the house to Mary for £250,000 as a way of reducing stamp duty from 3% to 1%. This is perfectly legal as stamp duty is paid on the *price* regardless of market value. John has in effect given Mary a gift of £20,000 in equity (the difference between £270,000 and £250,000). Should Mary later give John a new car, a financial gift or a payment in kind worth about £20,000, Mary would need to declare the gift to the tax authorities and offer to pay the stamp duty that would be due. In this example Mary would have to pay £5,600 in stamp duty (the difference between 3% of £270,000 and 1% of £250,000).

Example 6.

Father buys house for £190,000 *in his name* and gives it as a gift to his son. Father paid stamp duty (first stamp duty payment) when house purchased. Son paid no stamp duty when house received as a gift. Two years later (or two months later) the son mortgages the house and gives £190,000 to father. This must be declared to the tax authorities, as stamp duty would be liable (second stamp duty payment) on the payment of £190,000 to father. In this example, stamp duty has been paid twice. This can be avoided as follows: Instead of buying a house in his name, the father can buy the house in *his son's name* and pay stamp duty only once. Then at any time later, the son can mortgage the house and repay the father without any further stamp duty costs.

Example 7.

Angela owns a house with a market value of £240,000 and a mortgage of £150,000. She gives the house as a gift to Robert provided Robert takes over the mortgage. Robert must pay stamp duty on £150,000 even though the house was a gift because the outstanding mortgage is deemed to be a financial payment. Note that if at a future date Robert gives Angela any kind of reciprocal payment for the house gift, there will be a further stamp duty payment to make. Taking over any kind of outstanding mortgage is deemed to be a consideration.

Example 8.

Angela owns a house with a market value of £240,000 and a mortgage of £150,000. She sells her house to Robert for £90,000 on condition he takes over the mortgage. Robert has to pay stamp duty on the total of £150,000 plus £90,000. A property mortgage cannot be 'gifted' as a way of avoiding stamp duty.

These examples show that stamp duty can sometimes be avoided by gifting in legitimate ways that are fully sanctioned by the tax authorities.

It's also important to understand the capital gains tax consequences of gifting property. Detailed information is contained in the Taxcafe guide *How to Avoid Property Tax*.

Another important point relates to transactions involving companies and this is explained through the examples that follow.

Examples

1 John has a house in his name and he decides to gift the property to his company. There is anti-avoidance legislation which deems the gift to be at open market value because the gift is to a company and John is "connected to his company". As a result, John's Company will have to pay stamp duty based on the open market value of the property. Whether parties are connected is determined by applying the test in section 839 of the Income and Corporation Taxes Act 1988. In summary, section 839 provides that individuals are connected with their

143

spouses, relatives and their spouse's relatives. Persons acting together to control a company are connected with both one another and that company.

2 If, on the other hand, John's Company bought a property and paid the usual stamp duty on the acquisition of the property, and later the property is gifted to John, there will not be any stamp duty payable on the gift to John as there is no chargeable consideration. This is because the anti-avoidance rule applies only to gifts to a company, and not gifts from a company. However there would be direct tax consequences that would need to be considered.

3 Gifting of property between unconnected companies is unusual. By contrast, a gift or sale at undervalue between companies in a group is not uncommon. However, there is intra-group relief that allows companies under common ownership to transfer property around the group without triggering a charge to stamp duty. This relief is subject to strict conditions and there are claw-back provisions to prevent the exemption being exploited.

For a full definition of 'connected persons' see the *Income and Corporation Taxes Act 1988, section 839.* You can get a free copy on the internet by going to:
www.opsi.gov.uk/acts/acts1988/Ukpga_19880001_en_71.htm

(Alternatively type 'Income and Corporation Taxes Act 1988' into Google UK and click the link to www.opsi.gov.uk and scroll down to the link: '839 Connected Persons'.)

Here is a summary of the things to watch out for when making a property gift (residential or non-residential):

1. No stamp duty applies if the gift is between private individuals. This is so regardless of the relationship between the individuals. It does not matter whether the gift is between family members, spouses, or strangers. The tax authorities are not in the business of judging the nature of human relationships.

2. When a gift is made there must be no reciprocal payment in cash or in kind, otherwise stamp duty will apply.

3. Gifts by an individual to a company will attract stamp duty at the open market value if the parties are connected. Parties are connected, if the individual controls the company taking into account also the individual's spouse, relatives and their spouse's relatives.

4. If a property with a mortgage is gifted, the person taking over the mortgage must pay stamp duty on the value of that mortgage.

The Company Strategy

This strategy allows you to sell a residential or non-residential property of any value (and in any part of the UK) without any *Stamp Duty Land Tax* being paid to the tax authorities. And naturally, it is completely sanctioned and approved by Inland Revenue. Furthermore, the amount of stamp duty avoided can then be shared in any proportion desired, between Buyer and Seller.

The Company Strategy is based on the following principle:

When you *buy* a property you normally pay stamp duty at the applicable rate. Also, when you *sell* a property, the next Buyer will normally pay stamp duty at the applicable rate. This means *stamp duty is paid twice on the same property*: once on the purchase and once on the sale. *The Company Strategy* shows how *stamp duty is only paid once instead of twice!* In other words, stamp duty is paid on the purchase, but not on the sale.

This is how it works:

*   John (the Buyer) will form a company just for the purpose of buying a property. Having formed the company, John will then buy a property and pay the proper stamp duty in the usual way. So John now owns a company, and the company owns a property.

*   At some future date, when the property is offered for sale, John becomes the Seller. So the property is now offered for sale in the usual way. But John has a big card up his sleeve. He can offer the property 'stamp duty paid' with virtually no financial loss. John can do this because, instead of selling the property, he can sell the company that owns the property (when you do this virtually no stamp duty applies).

*   John sells the company by selling all the shares in the company to Peter, the new Buyer. The shares were sold to Peter at a total price equivalent to the price of the property. Peter also has to pay stamp duty when he buys the shares, but the rate is only 0.5%. So now Peter owns the company that

owns the property. The net result is that when the property was sold, the stamp duty rate was only 0.5% regardless of price.

• Peter now has the advantage that when he in turn comes to sell the property he has a ready-made company that owns the property and only 0.5% stamp duty will apply. However, if Peter wishes, he can sell the property in the conventional way, i.e. his company can sell the *property* to a Buyer instead of selling *shares* to a Buyer (in which case, the usual property stamp duty rate will apply).

At this point you may be thinking that this is too good to be true. And in fact you would be right to think this because there are in fact two catches. And because of these catches we are not making a big song and dance about this strategy. First we will look at the advantages of this strategy, and then the disadvantages.

Advantages

1. You can buy a property and, in effect, 'recover' the stamp duty when you sell it.

2. The cost of stamp duty is reduced to a maximum of 0.5% regardless of property value.

3. The Strategy can be applied to any value property in any part of the UK.

4. It is completely sanctioned and approved by Inland Revenue.

5. It is ideal for property professionals who buy and **sell** properties (not suitable if planning to keep property for long term).

Disadvantages

(Note: There are two catches, as explained below)

1. **The Company formation.** The protagonist (i.e. the person applying the strategy) will be forming a company exclusively for the ownership of the target property. This will be a non-trading company that owns just one asset, the target property.

The cost of forming a company varies between £20 and £200 depending on whether you do it yourself.

2. **The mortgage.** If the protagonist is buying the property with a mortgage, a company mortgage will be required because the property is being purchased in the name of a company. This should not be too much of a problem because company mortgages for property purchases are becoming more widely available in the UK.

3. **Catch no. 1 – Legal undertaking.** The Buyer will not be buying the target property. Instead, the Buyer will be buying the company that owns the target property. In this regard, the Buyer must instruct his solicitor to buy a company (rather than a property) from the protagonist, and ensure that full unencumbered ownership of the company is passed on to him, the Buyer. This requires the protagonist to give the Buyer a *watertight legal undertaking* that the company is unencumbered, has not traded, and has no claims against it, AND that should anybody make a claim against the company arising from a date before the company was sold, the protagonist will be personally liable. Giving this *legal undertaking* is no problem (and no risk) for the protagonist, but persuading the Buyer to accept the undertaking may be difficult. Also, there may be additional legal fees for arranging the *legal undertaking* as part of the property transaction.

4. **Catch no. 2 – Tax.** When the protagonist comes to sell the property he has two options:

   • **Option 1:** Abandon *The Company Strategy* and sell the property in the conventional way. That is, the Buyer would pay the full stamp duty applicable and buy the property from the protagonist's company. The company would remain under the ownership of the protagonist, but it would now own nothing except the proceeds of sale. The company would pay corporation tax on the capital gain and distributing the proceeds to the company owner would have additional tax consequences. It is very likely that the company owner would end up paying more in tax than if the property had never been put in a company.

   • **Option 2:** Apply *The Company Strategy* and sell the company shares to the Buyer as a way of transferring ownership of the company and the property to the new owner. Again the capital gains tax consequences would have to be examined carefully by the buyer and the seller (see the Taxcafe.co.uk guide *Using a Property Company to Save Tax* for more information). From a legal perspective the buyer may be nervous about acquiring a company instead of just a property. For example, he may fear that the company has unpaid bills or other debts that will become his responsibility. Although this issue can be taken care of in the contract governing the sale of the company, many buyers will probably still be reluctant to buy a company instead of a property.

This is not a strategy that we generally recommend, mainly because of the potential tax and legal ramifications.

The Back-to-Back Strategy

This strategy is for people who wish to buy a property and sell it on without potentially incurring the cost of stamp duty. It is particularly applicable if buying 'off-plan' i.e. before the property is built, and then selling the property before completion of purchase.

Normally, if you buy a property and then sell it at a later date, the stamp duty paid on purchase cannot be recovered. However, if you buy a property (whether off-plan, new, or not new) there is a way of avoiding stamp duty if you plan to sell it again.

The strategy is based on selling the property before completion of purchase. This is how it works:

Step 1: You find a property *but before you buy it* you ascertain a potential buyer or market for the property in question. For example, you buy a new flat 'off-plan' in a city centre and you are reasonably confident that in several months' time when the property is built you will be able to sell it on. Alternatively, you find a customer who is looking for a specific property – you then find that specific property and make it available to your customer.

Step 2: You buy the property to the extent that you pay a reservation fee or a deposit and you exchange contracts. At this stage you must make sure that you have an 'assignable contract' (i.e. a contract that allows you to sell the property on to another person without any penalties or legal repercussions). This should not be a problem as many property contracts, particularly off-plan purchases, are assignable. You are now 'committed' to buying the property whether or not you can find a customer to sell on to. Note that you have not yet completed the sale, i.e. you have not yet paid the full price.

Step 3: You find a customer who would like to buy the property instead of you. In this scenario you instruct your solicitor to do a 'back-to-back' transaction so that you can sell the property on to your customer without 'completion' on your part. Then, when your customer completes the purchase he will pay the stamp duty in the normal way. You paid no stamp duty at any point.

150

Back-to-back property deals where A sells to B, and B sells on to C have two advantages for party 'B':

- Stamp duty is avoided.

- Party 'B' is able to buy a property and sell it on without having to finance the transaction.

The tax authorities are quite happy for this kind of transaction to take place, provided that party 'B' does not *substantially perform*. If you *substantially perform* you will be fully liable to pay stamp duty. What does *substantially perform* mean?

According to the tax authorities, *substantially perform* means the following:

If you have *substantially performed* it means that as far as stamp duty is concerned you have completed the purchase and you have to pay stamp duty *even if the completion of purchase has not occurred yet*.

You are deemed to have *substantially performed* if you have done any of the following:

- Paid 90% or more of the property price.

- Taken possession of the property (e.g. have the keys).

- Paid any rent for the property.

- Carried out any works, alterations or renovations to the property.

However, there is no specified time period in the regulations. So provided you do not *substantially perform*, you can take as long as you like between reserving a property (or exchanging contracts) and finding a customer to sell on to. Naturally, you are likely to face time constraints imposed by the Seller, and at some point the completion of purchase would be expected to go ahead.

Clearly, *The Back-To-Back Strategy* is a strategy for property entrepreneurs as it carries an element of risk, i.e. the risk that a customer to sell on to at a profit will not be found. Therefore, you would pursue this strategy for the business potential, and the savings in stamp duty would be regarded as incidental.

The Threshold Strategy For Non-Residential Property

In PART ONE of this book we saw how you could avoid or minimize stamp duty in two basic ways:

1. By negotiating a better price if the selling price is over but near a stamp duty threshold. For example if the price is £260,000 it is possible that the price has been put up to this figure to 'get away' from the £250,000 threshold (in which case a good reduction could be negotiated). Alternatively, if a Seller has a house or shop worth £260,000 he can offer the property at £250,000 and arrange to sell a list of chattels for £10,000. This makes the property easier to sell and more attractive to a potential buyer as there will be less stamp duty to pay.

2. By fully exploiting 'chattels' (known as 'movables' in Scotland) to get a price reduction below a stamp duty threshold. Study this subject carefully in PART ONE as it is important to observe the legal niceties if using this strategy.

Regarding non-residential property, there are no differences in strategy except that the tax thresholds are different. Here is a comparison:

COMPARISON OF STAMP DUTY THRESHOLDS
(Only the first threshold is different)

Residential	Non-residential
Over £125,000 = 1%	Over £150,000 = 1%
Over £250,000 = 3%	Over £250,000 = 3%
Over £500,000 = 4%	Over £500,000 = 4%

So, for example, for non-residential property (using the same 'Threshold Strategy' as described in PART ONE of this book) you should look carefully at any selling prices between £151,000 and £170,000 to see if there is room for negotiation.

If chattels, equipment, machinery, commercial stock, or any kind of inventory are involved you may have a dilemma between choosing Scenario A or Scenario B as follows:

Scenario A

The Buyer could negotiate a selling price that includes chattels or commercial inventory. In this case the Lender pays for the chattels, albeit indirectly as strictly speaking commercial property loans are not meant to cover chattels. The advantage here is that the Buyer does not have to find cash to buy the chattels separately. The disadvantage is that if negotiating a price close to a stamp duty threshold the Buyer has less room for manoeuvre. That is, the Buyer will have less flexibility to use chattels as a way of getting the price reduced to a lower threshold.

Scenario B.

The Buyer could negotiate a selling price that does not include chattels or commercial inventory. In this case the Lender does not pay for the chattels (instead the Seller does). The advantage here is that the Buyer can negotiate a below-threshold price to minimize stamp duty. The disadvantage is that the Buyer has to find the cash to pay for the chattels.

Naturally, the choice of scenario A or B above is going to depend on the financial resources of the Buyer, the selling price, and the value of the chattels or commercial inventory.

For the Seller, the decision on whether to offer scenario A or B above depends on several factors:

Does the inventory add value to the business or commercial property being sold? If, for example, you are selling a newsagent's as a 'going concern' then clearly the inventory would be included. And there are Lenders who specialize in commercial mortgages that would include the inventory, the business goodwill, and so on.

On the other hand, if selling an office building, an empty shop, or a factory, there may be good reasons for selling the inventory separately to the mutual benefit of both Buyer and Seller.

The point is this: Always look at chattels, equipment and inventory in a non-residential property transaction to see how best to exploit the deal and minimize stamp duty.

The Link Strategy For Non-Residential Property

The Link Strategy in PART ONE of this book applies equally to non-residential and commercial property. However, as we saw in the previous strategy, the stamp duty thresholds are different, as shown below.

Comparison of Stamp Duty Thresholds
(Only the first threshold is different)

Residential	Non-residential
Over £125,000 = 1%	Over £150,000 = 1%
Over £250,000 = 3%	Over £250,000 = 3%
Over £500,000 = 4%	Over £500,000 = 4%

The Link Strategy is particularly effective with commercial property. This is because very often a commercial real-estate deal can involve more than one property. However, make sure you get good legal advice before you proceed to ensure that this strategy will work in your personal circumstances.

Clearly, if buying commercial property that includes an element of residential property they cannot be separated out so as to avoid linkage. For example, a flat above a shop, a home on a farm, or a live-in pub come to mind. In these situations you cannot split the residential element from the non-residential element as a way of creating two transactions to minimize stamp duty. The linkage for stamp duty purposes will always be there if sold to or bought from the same person or company.

A question that sometimes arises with commercial or residential property is *How do you deal with a portfolio of properties?* That is, how do you buy several properties from the same source without incurring the punitive 'linked transaction' rate of stamp duty?

This can arise when a business that owns several properties changes to new ownership, or when a person that owns a portfolio of properties wants to retire and divest himself of his properties.

The answer is to apply *The Link Strategy* as explained in PART ONE of this book. Again, always seek professional advice before you act.

The Land Strategy For Non-Residential Property

Land is regarded by the tax authorities as non-residential property. This is so even if the land being purchased is for residential purposes. The fact that you cannot reside on the land at that moment is what counts.

The rates of stamp duty for non-residential property are as follows:

Property Price	Stamp Duty
Not more than £150,000	0%
More than £150,000 but not more than £250,000	1%
More than £250,000 but not more than £500,000	3%
More than £500,000	4%

This means that if you are buying a plot of land to build a home, it is regarded as non-residential property and, as a consequence, no stamp duty applies if the price is not over £150,000.

This strategy can be used to avoid stamp duty if buying land or property for building or re-building purposes.

Clearly, this strategy is only suitable if you are contemplating buying a plot of land and building a property (residential or non-residential). One of the biggest problems faced by builders is 'planning permission'. It is not too difficult to buy land, but getting planning permission to build on the land is usually very difficult and sometimes impossible.

One solution is to buy a dilapidated property, a wreck, or an abandoned property as the land will already have 'planning permission' by virtue of the existing building. The existing building can then be demolished and a new building erected.

Naturally, fresh planning permission would need to be obtained but it is far more likely to be granted if a building already existed on the site.

Stamp duty can be avoided by not buying a 'property' as such – instead, you buy the 'land' it is standing on. By doing this, you pay no stamp duty up to a threshold of £150,000 (compared with a threshold of £125,000 for residential property). Here's an example:

An old abandoned bungalow is for sale at £140,000. It has a large garden, big enough to build a new house or a block of flats. Instead of buying the bungalow and paying £1,400 in stamp duty, you agree with the owner that you will buy the property as *land* at the same price of £140,000. By doing this you save £1,400 in stamp duty. In this example, it must be made clear to the Buyer's solicitor that the bungalow is *'no longer suitable as a dwelling and will not be used as such'*.

What's the catch? you may ask. Why not always buy a house as land and avoid stamp duty? The catch is that the property being purchased must not be a *'residential property'* or *'must not be suitable as a dwelling.'* This is how the tax authorities define a so-called *residential property*:

(Extract from the Finance Act 2003)

> *(a) A building that is used or suitable for use as a dwelling, or is in the process of being constructed or adapted for such use, and*
>
> *(b) Land that is or forms part of the garden or grounds of a building within paragraph (a) (including any building or structure on such land), or*
>
> *(c) An interest in or right over land that subsists for the benefit of a building within paragraph (a) or of land within paragraph (b).*

What does this definition really mean? It simply means that an old abandoned building that is <u>no longer suitable</u> for use as a dwelling (or for any other meaningful purpose) is not regarded as *residential property*. And that being the case, it can only be regarded as non-residential property.

Should you want to apply *The Land Strategy For Non-residential Property* and you have found a possible target property, the first step would be to get confirmation from your solicitor that the target property can in fact be purchased as a non-residential property. Alternatively, you may wish to explain to the Seller that he can obtain a better price for the property by having it demolished, thus making the land more attractive to buy. A heap of rubble is more likely to pass the *non-residential property* test than an abandoned wreck! Sometimes, you do not even have to demolish the property: it may be enough to just remove the roof, thus rendering the property as uninhabitable. You may then also avoid council tax costs.

A final thought on this subject: If you are looking for a plot of land to build on *and* be sure of getting planning permission, it may be worth buying a dilapidated property (and knocking it down) even if you have to pay stamp duty for the privilege.

The Price Strategy For Non-residential Property

As explained in PART ONE of this book, *The Price Strategy* is based on the following principle:

A Buyer and a Seller negotiate and agree a price reduction. The price reduction amount is given to the Buyer as a Cash Incentive. The money for the Cash Incentive originates from the Lender, but is paid to the Buyer via the Seller. That is why it is called a 'Cash Incentive'.

If you are not sure how this works please refer to *The Price Strategy* chapter in PART ONE of this book before proceeding.

The Price Strategy described in PART ONE also applies to land and commercial property in just the same way. The difference, of course, is that the property being bought or sold is classified as non-residential property, e.g. commercial property or land.

House building companies in the UK have been using *The Price Strategy* described in this book for many years, albeit packaged slightly differently. Hence, the practice of including a cash incentive in a property deal is a well-trodden road.

In applying *The Price Strategy For Non-residential Property* the following considerations should be taken into account:

1. If buying the property from a company it may not be enough to talk to a 'company representative'. Negotiations will need to be conducted with the true decision maker. If dealing with an estate agent it will be important to get past the agent and reach the decision-maker direct. If this is not possible, then negotiations can be conducted through the estate agent provided the agent is in contact with the decision-maker.

2. It does not matter whether a company is buying from a private individual, or a private individual buying from a company, or a company buying from a company. *The Price Strategy For Non-residential Property* is valid in all these permutations.

3. Step 3 in *The Price Strategy* (see PART ONE of book) requires a letter to be signed to indicate agreement in principle. If the land or commercial property being bought or sold belongs to a business, then any communications from that business should be on the letterhead of the business.

The Valuation Strategy For Non-Residential Property

As explained in PART ONE of this book, *The Valuation Strategy* is based on the following principle:

A Buyer and a Seller negotiate and agree an AMOUNT as payment for the property. Another higher figure is agreed as the SELLING PRICE based on comparable property. The difference between the AMOUNT and the SELLING PRICE is given to the Buyer as a Cash Incentive. The money for the Cash Incentive originates from the Lender, but is paid to the Buyer via the Seller/solicitor.

If you are not sure how this works please refer to *The Valuation Strategy* in PART ONE before proceeding.

The Valuation Strategy described in PART ONE also applies to land and commercial property in just the same way. The difference, of course, is that the property being bought or sold is classified as non-residential property, e.g. commercial property or land.

Note that if a residential property is being purchased (or sold) in the name of a company stamp duty is paid at the rate applicable to *residential* property.

In applying *The Valuation Strategy For Non-residential Property* the following considerations should be taken into account:

1. **Direct negotiations.** It may not be enough to talk to a 'company representative'. Negotiations will need to be conducted with the true decision-maker. If dealing with an estate agent it will be important to get past the agent and reach the decision-maker direct. If this is not possible, then negotiations can be conducted through the estate agent provided the agent is in contact with the decision-maker.

2. **Buying property in a company name.** It does not matter whether a company is buying from a private individual, or a private individual buying from a company, or a company buying from a company. *The Valuation Strategy For Non-residential Property* is valid in all these permutations.

162

3. **Written communications**. Step 3 in The Valuation Strategy (as explained in PART ONE of this book) requires two letters to be signed in principle (by the Buyer or Seller) to confirm details and to indicate a willingness to proceed. If the land or commercial property being bought or sold belongs to a business, then any communications from that business should be on the letterhead of the business.

4. **Comparable prices**. Comparables for some types of non-residential property may not be readily available in the locality. The way round this is go further away or use comparables that are not so physically similar. This is how Valuers and Estate Agents arrive at 'open market values' for non-residential property when there is no similar business/property nearby.

5. **The business**. Unlike residential property, non-residential property can sometimes include other things that add value to the total selling price. This can be the case when a whole business is being sold (not just the commercial property). For example, business goodwill, equipment and machinery, commercial inventory, trading history, business performance, and so on. When such factors are taken into account in arriving at an overall selling price, a comparable is sometimes not possible to find. However, the market value of, for example, the physical premises will be assessed separately for stamp duty purposes. Therefore a comparable for the building is what you are after, not a comparable for the business.

6. **Stamp duty assessment.** In assessing stamp duty on a non-residential property transaction, the tax authorities take into account three things: The selling price of the physical property, the fixtures and fittings, and the inherent goodwill. Let's look at each of these in turn.

   6.1 **Selling price of physical property**. Stamp duty is payable on the selling price agreed for the commercial property or land. Very often, when buying commercial property it may be part of a package of other goods and services. It is important, therefore, to separate the non-residential property-element of the contract so that this element is listed and priced separately in the contract.

   For example if buying a shop as a going concern, stamp duty is payable on the shop premises, but not the inventory. Another good example is a fish and chip shop: You don't pay stamp duty on the market value of the fryers. So when you buy a business you want to buy a 'shopping list' of separately priced items, one of which is the commercial property.

If this cost is not separated out there is a risk that the tax authorities will expect stamp duty to be paid on the whole cost of the business or *on their estimate* of 'the open market value' of the property.

Note that you are only interested in comparables if a mortgage applies and if, as a Buyer, you want a Cash Incentive out of the deal. If you are a Seller, you want to be able to offer a Cash Incentive to a Buyer as a way of securing a sale. The Cash Incentive can be used by the Buyer to pay for stamp duty and other costs that cannot normally be included in the mortgage.

6.2 **Fixtures and fittings.** Stamp duty is payable on fixtures and fittings (including commercial equipment and machinery *fixed* to or forming a part of the property/land) as they are regarded as 'inherent to the property'. There is no need to list fixtures and fittings separately – you simply include them in the price since there is no stamp duty advantage in separating them. You may, however, list the fixtures and fittings for the benefit of the Buyer and solicitor to avoid any misunderstandings over what is being sold. Fixtures and fittings cannot be purchased separately as a way of avoiding stamp duty or as a way of getting a price reduction. However, chattels (known as 'movables' in Scotland) *can be* purchased separately as a way of avoiding stamp duty, or as a way of getting a price reduction. Chattels and movables include the following:

- Any kind of goods, stock, office equipment, or commercial inventory so long as they are not physically fixed to the property.

- Any commercial intangibles such as skills, knowledge and expertise; trademarks, brands, and patents; assets such as vehicles and valuables; and any other items of value not physically attached to the property.

6.3 Inherent goodwill. Stamp duty is payable on 'inherent goodwill' but not on 'business goodwill'. The value of inherent goodwill is added to the value of the physical property for assessment purposes.

- **Inherent goodwill** is defined somewhat informally by the tax authorities (as it is a matter of 'interpretation') as being *'goodwill that is inherent to the physical location'* being sold. For example, a pub called 'Shakespeare' sited opposite the house where Shakespeare lived would benefit from custom by virtue of its business name in relation to its physical location (i.e. the customers or goodwill come to it because of its physical location). Another example might be a tourist shop close to Hadrian's Wall that specialized in Hadrian's Wall paraphernalia (the goodwill arises from its physical location). A football clothing shop close to a football stadium, or a boat shop next to a lake might be other examples.

- **Business goodwill** does not attract any stamp duty, and can be defined as an intangible asset, valued according to the advantage or reputation a business has acquired (over and above its tangible assets). The way to minimize stamp duty in a commercial transaction is to emphasize 'business goodwill' rather than 'inherent goodwill' (assuming this to be the case). Clearly, if inherent goodwill applies, then this should be mentioned as applicable.

- Try to keep the value of business goodwill as low as possible, perhaps by increasing the value of other chattels and movables to 'even things out'. That way, if the tax authorities want to argue that the business goodwill should be classified as inherent goodwill, the amount involved will not be so big. If it is clear that inherent goodwill will not apply, realize that business goodwill, chattels, and commercial inventory are factors that can be priced to advantage as a way of minimizing stamp duty.

Naturally you should always obtain professional advice before you act.

The Combination Strategy For Non-Residential Property

The Combination Strategy in PART ONE of this book shows how various strategies can be combined to good effect. In particular *The Price Strategy* and *The Valuation Strategy* go hand in hand and should always be considered together when trading in non-residential property. If anything, non-residential property gives greater scope than residential property for combining various strategies because of the higher nil-tax threshold (£150,000) and because of a greater variety of chattels and movables that might be available for negotiation.

For example, if buying a car repair shop the price could be negotiated below a tax threshold by offering to buy valuable car repair equipment that is not fixed to the property. If no such equipment is available, then a price could be paid for the *'Business Goodwill'* (there is no stamp duty on Business Goodwill). A Cash Incentive equivalent to the price reduction could also be obtained. For an even bigger Cash Incentive, the Buyer could try to get a good comparable. The point here is that all the ways of combining the strategies for residential property are equally valid for non-residential property.

Top 10 Ways to Get on The Property Ladder

If you're a first-time buyer or short of money, buying a property can be very difficult. In the UK most mortgage lenders require the Buyer to pay a deposit that is between 5% and 15% of the price. You can get 100% mortgages but this usually means accepting less favourable mortgage terms, such as a higher interest rate.

Saving enough money to pay for a deposit, legal fees, etc. is the main issue faced by most people. Given the price of property generally, a 10% deposit can easily amount to £10,000-£20,000. When on top of this you have to pay legal fees, stamp duty, and other costs, the total amount can seem insurmountable to many.

There are, however, several ways to buy property even if you do not have enough money to finance the deal. What follows are the ten best ways to do this, in no particular order. Although not related to stamp duty planning, these strategies will be of interest to all people involved in property. Some of the strategies that follow will be more suitable than others depending on your circumstances, and that is why no particular strategy is said to be 'better' than the others.

The top ten ways to get on the property ladder

1. Government grant strategy
2. Shared equity strategy
3. Build your own home strategy
4. Buy property abroad strategy
5. Property renovation strategy
6. The landlord strategy
7. Save every penny strategy
8. Relocation strategy
9. Buy with another person strategy
10. No money down strategy

1. GOVERNMENT GRANT STRATEGY.

Throughout the UK you can get special government assistance if you or a member of your household meets the qualification criteria. As taxpayers' money is being used, most government housing schemes are means tested or based on the type of occupation you do.

For example, in England there is a 'Key Worker Scheme' (also known as the 'Key Worker Living Programme'). This is a Government initiative to provide affordable accommodation for people who work within a specified group of occupations in the public sector where there is shortage of employment retention due to travel and housing affordability in that area. The main schemes open to key workers are Shared Ownership, Homebuy and Intermediate rent.

To qualify, at least one member of the household must be employed within a specified 'Key Worker' group.

A Key Worker is someone

- employed by the public sector

- in a frontline role delivering an essential public service

- in a sector where there are serious recruitment and retention problems.

If you are a Key Worker in one of the groups listed below you could get help (i) to buy your first home (Homebuy), (ii) to part-rent/part-buy a home (Shared Ownership), or (iii) to move into a rented home, which you may later be able to buy. The list that follows is not exhaustive as they can include a variety of more detailed sub groups.

- Health Workers (NHS staff including Social Workers etc).

- Teachers, including physical education teachers.

- Prison officers and some Prison Service staff.

- Probation Officers, Senior Probation Officers, Probation Service. Officers and Trainee Probation Officers.

- Social workers (N.B only qualified Social Workers who have attained the recognised professional Social Worker Degree/Diploma are eligible – not trainees or unqualified staff).

- Educational psychologists, occupational, language, and speech therapists (must be fully qualified – trainees are not eligible).

- London Planners.

- Fire and Rescue workers.

- Police Officers and Police civilian workers.

The aim of the *Key Worker scheme* is to make buying your first home that bit easier and includes the following types of help:

- Loans of up to £50,000 towards buying a home

- Loans of up to £100,000 for London school teachers who have the potential to become leaders of London's education system

- Shared ownership of new properties

In England if you do not quality as a 'Key Worker' you may still qualify for a government grant if you can pass the government's means test under the 'Homebuy' scheme.

The 'Homebuy' scheme helps eligible people to buy a home on the open market who could not afford to do so without assistance. It is funded by the Housing Corporation, a government body that has responsibility for registered social housing landlords in England.

Under the 'Homebuy' model, purchasers receive an interest-free loan of 25% of the purchase price of their home (by contrast, the Shared Ownership model offers 'part rent, part buy'). 'Homebuy' is often preferred to shared ownership options because of the lack of rent payments on the 25 per cent balance of the property's value and the greater sense of 'ownership'. Also, 'Homebuy' is much more attractive to mortgage lenders because of the absence of a lease between the purchaser and the registered social landlord.

The 'Homebuy' scheme is available throughout England, and the *Key Worker Scheme* is available mainly in London and south-east England. However, similar schemes (sometimes referred to as 'Affordable Housing' or 'Low Cost Home-Ownership Schemes') are available in other parts of the UK. To find out more here are some useful contacts:

England	Phone: 0845 300 2820 Web site: *www.keyworkerliving.co.uk.* Also try: *www.direct.gov.uk/HomeAndCommunity/fs/en* For Homebuy go to *www.housingcorp.gov.uk* Phone 0845 230 7000.
Wales	Phone: 029 20 825111 Web site: *www.wales.gov.uk/index.htm* (click 'H' in the index for 'Housing')
Scotland	Phone: 0845 7 741741 or 0131 556 8400 Web site: *www.scotland.gov.uk/Home* (click on 'Housing and regeneration'). Note: In Scotland 'Homestake' is a new low cost home ownership scheme, details of which can be found at: *www.communitiesscotland.gov.uk/stellent/groups/public/documents/webpages/cs_008156.hcsp*
Northern Ireland	Phone: 0289031 7000 Web site: *http://northernireland.shelter.org.uk/advice* For general contact information related to housing go to *www.nihe.gov.uk/addresses*, then click on an area of the map to get further information

2. SHARED EQUITY STRATEGY

This strategy is based on buying a property in association with the Government which becomes a part owner. Shared equity ownership schemes (also known as 'shared ownership schemes') are widely available throughout the UK and are typically managed through so-called 'Housing Associations'. Their core activity is to provide affordable housing through shared ownership and rental schemes.

As taxpayer's money is used by the Government to fund Housing Associations, you are normally means tested to determine if you qualify for a shared equity scheme.

Basically, *shared equity* is aimed at helping people in housing need who are unable to purchase a property on the open market. Priority is usually given to existing tenants and households on waiting lists for social housing.

In the March 2006 Budget the Government announced that it intends to extend home ownership to another one million people over the years 2006 - 2011, and to this end it will work with house builders, housing associations, and others to develop social housing needs. Generally, the government of the day is keen to promote shared equity schemes as this reduces the burden of Housing Benefit costs.

Although there is no shared equity scheme that exists nationwide, each region has its own scheme. In England, for example, purchasers of shared property can buy between 25% and a maximum of 75% of the property, and pay rent on the portion not owned. In Scotland this is what the Cairn Housing Association says:

'The initial purchase may be 25, 50 or 75% of the value of the property, with a rent being charged on the remaining portion. After the first year the applicant can increase the proportion owned in 25% shares (known as tranches) at any time or can purchase outright. Further details on Shared Ownership as a housing option are available from the Association or from the national housing agency, Communities Scotland.'

In Wales the *Wales & West Housing Association* says: *'shared ownership properties are sold to applicants on our waiting list who can support a small mortgage, but do not have sufficient funds to purchase on the open market. This allows applicants to purchase a share of the property, starting from 40%. When tenants can afford to purchase a larger share, they can "staircase" to full ownership in units of 20% shares.'*

So wherever you live, you should make local enquiries into the availability of Government sponsored shared equity schemes, as they vary from region to region.

The table that follows provides some starting points for finding out more information:

England	Phone: 0845 230 7000 Web site: *www.housingcorp.gov.uk*
Wales	Phone: 029 20 825111 Web site: *www.wales.gov.uk/index.htm* (click 'H' in the index for 'Housing')
Scotland	Phone: 0845 7 741741 or 0131 556 8400 Web site: *www.scotland.gov.uk/Home* (click on 'Housing and regeneration'). Also see *www.co-ownership.org* for 'co-ownership advice'.
Northern Ireland	Phone: 0289031 7000 Web site: *http://northernireland.shelter.org.uk/advice* Also see *www.co-ownership.org* for 'co-ownership advice'.

3. BUILD YOUR OWN HOME STRATEGY.

A variety of housing schemes exist that allow people to build their own home and as a consequence become a part-owner. Typically, you would own a quarter or a third of your home if participating in such a scheme. The big advantage is that you usually do not have to finance the building project to any significant level. The 'price' you pay is your time, i.e. the time spent in supervising and building the property.

Describing the variety of self-build schemes available in the UK is beyond the scope of this book, and furthermore such schemes are always changing depending on the building projects in hand. Here is an example of a typical scheme:

Several people join an association to build their own homes in a given location. They all join forces so that everybody works on every house until they are all complete. In return for giving their time to the project, everybody gets to be a 25% owner of their brand new home. Anytime they like they can buy a bigger percentage of their home. Once the homes are built, the properties are allocated to the participants, based on a random draw. This ensures that

172

while you are building the homes you do not know which home will end up being yours. This kind of scheme ensures there are always enough people available for building work, and no preference is given to any particular house.

Building your own home is an industry in itself. There are 'Housing Associations' that just do this. Also, there are mortgage companies who specialize in the *build-your-own-home* market. You can even buy magazines entirely devoted to the subject.

The government of the day is usually keen to encourage people to build their own homes because there is a chronic shortage of new housing in the UK. As a consequence, a variety of grants and self-help groups exist that make it possible for just about anyone to build their own home, even when money is short and you have no building skills. All you need is time and determination, and a willingness to help do the physical building work.

Clearly, the biggest incentive for somebody contemplating building their own home is the opportunity to own or part-own a property that you can enjoy and live in, knowing that it is likely to go up in value in the years to come (and give you a handsome profit should you ever sell).

Building your own home is a way to get a home which may meet all your needs and may cost considerably less than buying a ready-built house.

Financing this type of work can go along two routes:

A. Join a housing association, self-build group, or other co-operative house-building scheme with a view to getting a grant or a part-ownership in a property.

B. Get a self-build mortgage for building and owning 100% of your home. More risks are involved in building your own home but self-build mortgages can help with the financial complications of managing such a project. The main difference between a self-build mortgage and a house purchase mortgage is that with a self-build mortgage, money is released in *stages* as the build progresses (rather than as a single amount).

There are two types of self-build mortgages: (i) a traditional arrears-based mortgage released in staged payments, and (ii) an advance payment scheme that releases funds in advance of each stage of construction and removes the need for bridging loans. If

173

you want to stay in your current home while the new one is built, you will need to find out what the lender's attitude will be to any outstanding mortgage on your existing property.

About 20,000 people build their own homes in the UK each year and this number is rising. Over 30 banks and building societies offer mortgages to self-builders. You may be able to get between 25% and 80% of the value of the building plot and between 65% and 95% of the costs of the building.

If you want to take this further a good first step is to do some research on the internet or in your local reference library. The following website offers lots of information: *www.direct.gov.uk* (enter 'self-build' or 'build your own home' in the search box or see the index). Also try telephoning a main reference library and ask for 'self-build groups' in the geographical area you are interested in. Also have a look at specialist magazines on the subject.

4. BUY PROPERTY ABROAD STRATEGY.

If you are short of money for buying a property in the UK, buying abroad can be a good alternative. Property prices in places like Bulgaria, Poland, Cyprus, Slovenia, Estonia and other parts of Europe can be less than half compared with the UK (for a similar kind of property). And provided you carry out due diligence before buying, the risks are likely to be low.

It is not being suggested that you live abroad (unless you wish to). But buying abroad will get you 'on the property ladder' and you can benefit from rental income and property price appreciation.

The key to buying abroad is to decide whether you will be letting the property to *tourists* or to *business people*. If the former, the location needs to be in a tourist resort such as near a popular beach. If the latter, the location needs to be in a city centre where there is a growing demand from an existing business community. Do not fall into the trap of trying to cater for both markets – it never works. Also, it helps to be clear whether you are catering to people who are native to the country or to foreigners, as this will determine the type of estate agency to employ.

Once you have decided which country and which rental market to go for, you can start searching for a suitable property.

174

Finding finance for a foreign home is not as difficult as you might think. However, most British mortgage companies and banks will not be able to lend money unless they have subsidiaries or associates in the target country.

Fortunately, this is now changing - Halifax, for example, owns *Banco Halifax España*; Norwich & Peterborough Building Society has lending capabilities in Gibraltar and southern Spain and Barclay Bank has operations in France, Spain and Portugal. Other UK banks, including HSBC, have relationships with overseas lenders. Alternatively, you could use a local lender. They will consider mortgages on local properties regardless of your nationality.

If a British broker is used to arrange the mortgage, you won't have a language barrier even if the loan comes from an overseas lender. Firms such as *Conti Financial Services* and *Property Finance 4 Less* specialize in finding mortgages for British people using local lenders and British subsidiaries. Conti Financial, for example, sources mortgages in 20 countries.

As in the UK, the amount you can borrow will be capped at a maximum loan to value (LTV). As a general rule, overseas lenders require a larger deposit - often 75%-85% LTV. The point here is that as you are buying property that is cheaper than in the UK, the deposit requirement is likely to be lower even though the deposit percentage may be higher.

Here are some tips on buying property abroad:

- **Watch out for that hard sell under the sun**

  Many estate agents and property companies offer so called 'inspection flights'. Such flights are usually free or very cheap, and are offered because it is known that people usually do not buy property without first visiting the area. Some inspection flights can be an inexpensive way of finding a bargain property abroad. But others will be nothing less than 48 hours of hard sell with you as a captive audience. Another factor is that some inspection visits will show only the best homes in the best locations, include free meals with plenty of alcohol during the stay and thus create a feel-good atmosphere in which it becomes difficult for buyers to make

175

objective decisions. So if you want to accept an inspection flight, go ahead and enjoy it, but do it with your eyes open.

- **Watch your tax liability**

  Be wary about setting up an offshore company to own the property abroad. Some financial experts warn that doing this can actually increase your tax liability with Inland Revenue – you should seek expert advice before doing this.

  The Inland Revenue may seek to charge income tax on what it regards as a benefit in kind, namely your rent-free enjoyment of the holiday home. This is not an issue where the property is owned personally, but it could be where the legal owner is a company controlled by you.

  For overseas properties, the measure of the 'benefit' is the property's annual rental value in the local market. If you own a house worth £200,000, which has an annual rental value of £10,000, the Inland Revenue could seek tax on £10,000 at your marginal rate of tax. Naturally, this does not arise if you are renting the property out.

- **Find a good agent**

  Finding an estate agent you're happy with can really ease the process of purchasing abroad, especially if you're buying in an area with which you're not very familiar. You need to feel confident that the agent is not palming you off with properties the natives wouldn't touch with a bargepole. It is essential that they know what kind of place you're looking for and that they understand the needs of a buyer who cannot turn up for viewings at the drop of a hat.

  Ask the agent for proof that they are members of relevant professional bodies and don't sign anything until you've checked it out with a suitably qualified, English-speaking lawyer.

  In some countries buyers and sellers normally split the cost of estate agents fees (e.g. Italy) which can total around 6% of the purchase price. But where this is not the case be aware that the estate agent will usually be acting for the Seller rather than you, the Buyer

Many British people buying abroad opt for a dedicated English-speaking agent, often web-based, whose business is geared specifically to UK buyers. It is common for expatriates with good local knowledge and contacts to set up such agencies, frequently focusing on a particular region or a new market, like Bulgaria, Croatia and Turkey.

These firms often work hand in hand with local agents. They may simply share the commission but will normally charge extra, and frequently sell themselves as a 'one-stop shop', offering to link you up with everyone you need, from 'Brit-friendly' lawyers to architects, swimming pool suppliers and lettings management firms. Plenty of buyers have nothing but good things to say about such agents, and some claim that without them they would not have bought.

Like domestic UK estate agents, these firms are generally self-regulating. Personal recommendations, gut instincts and a good lawyer are the best protection; look out also for members of the *Federation of Overseas Property Developers and Agents*, which operates a code of ethics and can expel any member that breaks it.

- **Use a 'subject to survey' clause.**

In many parts of the world property surveys are much less of a tradition than in the UK, and British buyers can encounter negativity from vendors on the basis that a house has been standing for several hundred years and should therefore be bought 'as seen'.

It is somewhat rare for sellers to agree to a 'subject to survey' clause in purchase contracts; they are likely to insist on keeping the house on the market while the survey is carried out and you'll have to be a tough negotiator to secure a discount because of any faults you've found. Therefore you may need to be firm when offering to buy with a 'subject to survey' clause in the purchase contract.

- **Find a good lawyer.**

Use an English-speaking lawyer who has experience of the property market you are buying into. This can be a lawyer who is UK based with associates in the target country, or a

177

lawyer who is based in the target country. Make sure the lawyer trawls through all documentation to your satisfaction.

So long as you take sensible precautions, appoint trustworthy agents and get everything properly translated, your purchase has every chance of running smoothly. Above all, make sure you understand the step-by-step process of buying a property in your chosen country (e.g. the sequence of payments, the exchange of contracts procedure, and the legal and financial consequences should the buyer or seller pull out of the deal at any point).

5. PROPERTY RENOVATION STRATEGY.

Whole books have been written on the subject of property renovation. It basically involves buying a property at well below market price by virtue of its condition. The point here is that the property will be more 'affordable' given its condition, making it possible to become a property owner.   But perhaps more importantly, you have the opportunity of making a handsome profit by renovating a property and selling at a profit.

If you are starting out with little cash you should keep in mind that it may not be possible to get a mortgage for some properties because of their poor condition. If you are presented with such a case one way round it is to get a bank loan instead of a property mortgage.

To get such a bank loan will require you to treat the property renovation project as a *business*. Thus you would need to prepare a proper business plan and present it to the bank manager as a business proposal rather than as a mortgage application. The rate of interest on a business loan is likely to be less favourable than a mortgage, but this is a good way of starting. Ideally, you want to get the bank loan lined up before you start searching for a renovation project – that way you have the flexibility of buying at auction should you need to.

Also, note that when buying at auction you usually have to pay a 10% deposit there and then, should your auction bid be successful. Because of this you can get mortgages or loans that are tailored to the property auction market.   To find out more speak to a mortgage broker or do a search on the internet by entering:

'mortgage property finance'. Alternatively, telephone the property auction organizers to see if they can suggest a suitable lender that specializes in property auctions.

Some people find it convenient to live in the property they are renovating, others prefer not to. Every renovation project is unique and different; nevertheless, property renovators face many common issues which are summarized below.

- **The property.** Find a friendly builder who can evaluate a property for you as the first step. You want to get a rough idea about renovation costs. Also, you want to know about any hidden or major property defects. If you are short-listing several possible properties it may not be financially viable to pay for a string of professional surveys. You can either learn how to do this yourself, or pay an experienced builder for an hour of his time to walk round the property with you, while you take notes. It is not being suggested that you avoid getting a professional survey, I am simply pointing out possible alternatives. It is not difficult to learn how to assess the condition of a property, and there are books and courses on the subject. Clearly, if there is any possibility of a serious structural defect, you will need to get professional advice before proceeding.

- **The plan.** You must decide from the outset whether you are going to live in the property once finished, sell it, or rent it. This is important as it determines your business plan, time scales, financing, and so on.

- **The market.** It is essential to know the market *before* you buy a renovation property. You need to know in advance the maximum market value of the property once renovated, the market demand for such a property, the type of buyer you are catering to (executive, family, bachelor, etc.), and whether you will be dressing the house with furniture for presentation purposes. A good tip is to talk to local estate agents.

- **The auction.** Become familiar with property auctions. You can do this by attending auctions, studying their property catalogues, and by using the internet to research the subject. You may also find it helpful to subscribe to a publication like 'Property Auction News' (*www.propertyauctionnews.co.uk*, telephone 0170 982 0033).

- **The skills.** Learn the skills of property renovation by reading relevant books. This does not mean you have to know how to be a builder or a plumber. It's more about knowing how to manage a building project, how to co-ordinate the work, and how to work to a budget.

6. THE LANDLORD STRATEGY.

Getting a mortgage to buy your own home can sometimes be more difficult (financially) than getting a buy-to-let mortgage. This is so because to get a home loan you have to prove you are earning enough money to meet the monthly mortgage payments.

With a buy-to-let mortgage the Lender needs to know that you will get enough rent to pay the mortgage, and your earnings are less relevant. So if you are out of work or on a low income, you may find it easier to become a landlord compared with buying your own home.

In the recent past, buy-to-let mortgages typically required a bigger deposit (15% to 20%) compared with home loans. But this is changing because now you can get 90% loan-to-value mortgages for buy-to-let.

Another consideration is whether to get an interest-only mortgage or a repayment mortgage. Most landlords opt for interest-only mortgages because the monthly mortgage payments will be lower.

Usually, the purpose in becoming a landlord is to profit from property appreciation rather than trying to make a profit from rental income. You therefore want to buy property that is going to increase in value in the years to come.

Investing in property offers a unique factor not found in other types of investments such as stock and shares, antiques, art, or just about anything else. This unique factor is referred to as *'gearing'*. Here's an example:

Let's say you have £20,000 in bank savings which you decide to use as a deposit on a house worth £200,000. If the property goes up 5% in a year, you have made an unrealized profit of £10,000. But if you had kept the £20,000 savings in the bank instead of buying a property, you would have made only £1,000 'profit', assuming 5% interest. In this simple example, even if property

180

prices go up just 1% in a year you would still make £2,000 profit compared with £1,000 profit on the bank savings at 5%. The power of gearing is the real reason for investing in property.

7. SAVE EVERY PENNY STRATEGY.

Whichever strategy you may use to buy a property, you may still be short of money for the mortgage deposit. Below are some tips on saving money for your deposit. You need to be creative and determined to find ways to save, knowing that it won't be forever! When you have to be a Scrooge, let people know why you are saving.

- Sacrifice holidays and other leisure activities that require significant or regular expenditure. This is about changing your lifestyle for as long as it takes, to save the money you need.

- Make a *'Savings List'* of all the little ways can save money by thinking hard about your daily life (cheaper shopping, no luxuries, take packed lunch to work, cancel the gym subscription, spend less on leisure activities, etc.). Add as much as you can to the *Savings List* and use it each day to remind you how to save money. With time the savings will quickly add up to a tidy sum.

- Liquidize your assets. Do you have anything that you don't need and which could be sold? Review all your belongings and plan a strategy for selling disposable assets for maximum gain. Use cheap or free classified advertisements, boot sales, or the internet (Ebay) as ways to sell goods.

- Work part-time or longer hours. Can you add a part-time job to your life? Or can you get paid for overtime work in your current occupation? This could be a good solution for some people.

8. RELOCATION STRATEGY.

Consider buying a property in a cheaper location. Property prices can vary considerably, even in the same town or city. Check property advertisements in different areas and talk to estate agents to find out the cheapest locations that are within commuting distance of your work.

The cost of commuting to work by train or car can be very high, but this may still be more economical than buying a property in a more expensive area. Alternatively, consider changing jobs so that you can live where property is not so expensive.

Annual season tickets for long-distance train commuting can cost about £5,000, but you may be able to save more than this by paying for a mortgage based on £200,000 instead of £350,000. Additionally you get on to the property ladder and you benefit from capital appreciation.

If your work can be done from home and is not dependent on a geographic location, then relocating may not be so difficult. But if you go out to work you may consider combining the two: look for a property in a cheaper area and simultaneously look for a job in that same area.

9. BUY WITH ANOTHER PERSON STRATEGY.

This is a great strategy that is becoming increasingly popular as the first step on to the property ladder. This involves buying a property with a friend, relative, or partner (it should ideally be somebody that you know and can trust).

By joining forces with another person you only need to pay half the deposit and half the mortgage interest. Furthermore, when applying for a mortgage the amount you can borrow will be based on your combined income, giving you much greater scope for borrowing the amount you need.

Here are some tips on buying property with another person:

- **Mortgage broker.**

  Go together to a mortgage broker and explain that you both want to buy and share a property. Ask the broker to shortlist two or three possible mortgages that would suit your circumstances. Then get agreement in principle that the lender will be willing to grant a mortgage. Only then start looking for a property, knowing that you can buy jointly, and how much you can borrow.

- **Tenants in common.**

In the context of sharing the ownership of a property, it is preferable to buy a property as *'tenants in common'*. This is better than buying as *'joint tenants'* or 'joint owners' because *'tenants in common'* provides greater legal flexibility in the event that the arrangement to share a property comes to an end.

If you own your home as *joint tenants* then both of you own the whole of the property, so when one partner dies, the other automatically becomes the sole owner of the home. With *tenants in common*, you each own a share of the property, typically split half and half. So should one partner die as a *tenant in common*, his share would go into his estate rather than being inherited by the partner that owns the other half of the property.

- **Tenants in common agreement.**

It is advisable to create a *tenants in common agreement* (between the two parties buying the property) that spells out what to do if either party dies or wants to terminate the property-share arrangement. Such an agreement can also specify that both parties are equally responsible for maintenance and repair costs, buildings insurance, council tax, and other costs affecting the property as a whole. The *tenants in common agreement* should be a legal document drawn up by a qualified solicitor. Note that this agreement does not involve the lender or mortgage company.

Here are some examples of possible areas of conflict: if two brothers are *tenants in common*, what do you do if brother A wants to get married and move out? Or suppose brother B wants to sell the property but brother A is not willing to sell? Or suppose brother A dies, does brother B get first option to buy half the property from brother A's estate? Or suppose brother A loses his job and stops paying his half-share of the mortgage, where does that leave brother B?

Although such issues may never occur, it is important to have an agreement in place to resolve any possible points of conflict. It also provides peace of mind for all concerned.

10. NO MONEY DOWN STRATEGY.

This involves buying a property in a way that does not require the Buyer to pay the full amount of the deposit. Sometimes, it is even possible to pay no money at all for the deposit depending on how the property deal is structured. Buying a property with 'no money down' requires a combination of two elements: a *low deposit mortgage* and a *cash incentive*.

A low deposit mortgage simply refers to mortgage deals that require no more than, say, 5% deposit (or 10% at most). A mortgage broker can help a Buyer identify such mortgages, a task that should be carried out before searching for a property to buy.

Now we come to 'Cash incentives'. Many property deals offer the Buyer the potential opportunity for getting a large cash incentive. Think of a cash incentive as a 'cashback', i.e. you borrow X amount from a mortgage company and some of this borrowed money *comes back* to you as a cash incentive that can finance the mortgage deposit, legal fees, stamp duty, etc.

A cash incentive can typically amount to 5% of the price of the property. For example, if a 10% deposit is required (90% LTV mortgage), half of the deposit can be funded from the 5% cash incentive. Alternatively, the deposit required for a 95% LTV mortgage deal could be entirely financed from a 5% cash incentive.

Where does the cash incentive come from? Ultimately, the actual money for the cash incentive comes from the money borrowed to buy the property. But the Lender does not give a cash incentive to a Buyer by adding it to the mortgage. Instead, the cash incentive is taken from the amount of money borrowed to buy the property.

This has been practised for many years by large building companies who offer cash incentives for buying new homes. But anybody can use this strategy for buying any type of property. Furthermore, the Buyer would declare the cash incentive on his mortgage application form so there is nothing underhand about this strategy.

The cash incentive goes from the lender (the mortgage company) to the Buyer along the following route:

Lender ▶ Buyer's solicitor ▶ Seller's solicitor ▶ Back to Buyer's solicitor ▶ Buyer

This is why it is called a 'cash incentive'. The Seller is 'giving' the Buyer a sum of money (through his solicitor) as an incentive to buy the property (to finance redecorating or other improvements that may be required).

The Buyer benefits from a cash incentive in several ways:

- He gets to buy the property instead of losing it.

- He is able to get a mortgage because the deposit can be paid.

- He is able to get a mortgage on better terms than a 100% mortgage (assuming a 100% mortgage is even available).

Naturally, a cash incentive will make the amount borrowed a little higher than otherwise. But this could be preferable to failing to get the type of mortgage you want, or failing to buy a property that you have found.

So how do you get a cash incentive out of a property deal? This has already been answered in *PART ONE* of this book. So the reader is now urged to study the last three chapters in *PART ONE* which fully explain how to get a cash incentive when buying property. Please see the following three strategies in *PART ONE*:

- The Price Strategy

- The Valuation Strategy

- The Combination Strategy

Once you start looking for a property, be prepared to use any aspect of the above three strategies to get as much cash out of the deal as you can. In parallel with this talk to a mortgage broker and make sure you have an offer of a mortgage in principle, based on a 95% or 90% LTV mortgage. By knowing what mortgage you can get, and by understanding how to negotiate a cash incentive with a Seller, you will be well equipped to buy a property with little or no 'money down'.

Need Affordable & Expert Tax Planning Advice?

Try Our Unique Question & Answer Service

The purpose of this guide is to provide you with detailed guidance on how to pay less Stamp Duty on your property investments.

Ultimately you may want to take further action or obtain advice personal to your circumstances.

Taxcafe.co.uk has a unique online tax advice service that provides access to highly qualified tax professionals at an affordable rate.

No matter how complex your question, we will provide you with detailed tax planning guidance through this service. The cost is just £69.95.

To find out more go to **www.taxcafe.co.uk** and click the Tax Questions button.

Pay Less Tax!

... with help from Taxcafe's unique tax guides and software

All products available online at www.taxcafe.co.uk

> **How to Avoid Property Tax** - Essential reading for property investors who want to know all the tips and tricks to follow to pay less tax on their property profits.

> **Using a Property Company to Save Tax** - How to massively increase your profits by using a property company... plus all the traps to avoid.

> **How to Avoid Inheritance Tax** - A-Z of inheritance tax planning, with clear explanations and numerous examples. Covers simple and sophisticated tax planning.

> **Tax Planning for Couples** - How married and unmarried couples can save thousands in income tax, capital gains tax, inheritance tax and national insurance using a variety of powerful tax planning techniques.

> **Non Resident & Offshore Tax Planning** - How to exploit non-resident tax status to reduce your tax bill, plus advice on using offshore trusts and companies.

> **The World's Best Tax Havens** – How to cut your taxes to zero and safeguard your financial freedom.

> **How to Avoid Stamp Duty** - Little known but perfectly legal trade secrets to reduce your stamp duty bill when buying or selling property.

> **Grow Rich with a Property ISA** - Find out how to invest in property tax free with an ISA.

- ➤ **Using a Company to Save Tax** - Everything you need to know about the tax benefits of using a company to run your business.

- ➤ **Bonus vs Dividend** - Shows how shareholder/directors of companies can save thousands in tax by choosing the optimal mix of bonus and dividend.

- ➤ **How to Avoid Tax on Your Stock Market Profits** - How to pay less capital gains tax, income tax and inheritance tax on your stock market investments and dealings.

- ➤ **Selling a Sole Trader Business** - A potential minefield with numerous traps to avoid but significant tax-saving opportunities.

- ➤ **How to Claim Tax Credits** - Even families with higher incomes can make successful tax credit claims. This guide shows how much you can claim and how to go about it.

- ➤ **Property Capital Gains Tax Calculator** - Unique software that performs complex capital gains tax calculations in seconds.

Printed in the United Kingdom
by Lightning Source UK Ltd.
111229UKS00001B/187-348